FROM WORLDLY TO CHRISTIAN WISDOM AND TRUTH

FROM WORLDLY TO CHRISTIAN WISDOM AND TRUTH

All Ages

This book contains some essential steps and guidelines which can assist you in making the transformation from a worldly life to a Godly life in Christ Jesus. Also embodied within the pages of this book are techniques and principles which can successfully and effectively enable you to navigate this transition.

"From Worldly, To Christian Wisdom and Truth: My friend, receive your transformation. God bless you!"

Yours truly

Mr. Nicholas C. Charles

Order this book online at www.trafford.com
or email orders@trafford.com

Most Trafford titles are also available at major online book retailers.

Printed in the United States of America.

ISBN: 978-1-4669-0639-6 (sc)
ISBN: 978-1-4669-0640-2 (hc)
ISBN: 978-1-4669-0641-9 (e)

Library of Congress Control Number: 2011962184

Trafford rev. 10/19/2012

 www.trafford.com

North America & international
toll-free: 1 888 232 4444 (USA & Canada)
phone: 250 383 6864 ◆ fax: 812 355 4082

CONTENTS

Introduction vii

Factors to Consider When You Have Accepted Christ ix

1 : What Is True Marriage? 1

2 : What is the History of Marriage? 8

3 : God's Statement and Advice 19

4 : Marriage Is a Covenant. That's Why It Should
    Come From the Heart! 24

5 : What Is Marital Fidelity? 30

6 : The Basic Principle to Make Your Family Live Happily! 39

7 : Many Pastors Don't Speak With the Authority from
    God That Influences Men 52

8 : God is real; Let No One tell you otherwise. He
    Is the Creator of Heavens and Earth and All Things 61

9 : It is Not Right to Get Even, Why? 66

10 : Do You Always Want to Be First? Humility and
     Hospitality, get it! 72

11 : Does God Approve Of Those Parties Today? 77

12 : Christian, Will All Good People Be Saved? 82

13 : The Power and Influence of Music Lucifer Was
     In Charge Of the Music in Heaven 87

14 : Is Abortion Right? 111

15 : Church, a Godly View of Life! 119

16 : What Is the Worship That God Approves?

      Are all religions pleasing to God? 123

17 : How Can I Have Confidence In Myself? 132

18 : Immoral Dressing, What, I Can Wear? 138

19 : Will Sex Improve Your Relationship? 143

20 : My Friend, You Need, To Stand Firm in

      Temptation Times! 150

About the Messenger 167

Acknowledgment 171

Bibliography 175

INTRODUCTION

From Worldly, to Christian Wisdom and Truth, contains **values** for **new**born Christians who have **given their lives to Christ Jesus. New believers need to be taught basic principles needed to live righteously in this present world.** This book would enable you to discern what is right or wrong and how to apply Godly standards to your daily living.

Therefore, what you did in your pre-Christian life will be supernaturally changed. **This book is also dedicated to everyone who may be in darkness and have not yet surrendered their life to Christ Jesus,** whose glory will illuminate their lives thereby enabling them to truly become over-comers. **My friend, attending fetes and parties, listening to ungodly music, participating in ungodly entertainment, or being a lover of money** more than a lover of God are doors which can lead you into compromising positions.

However, an understanding of the doctrines of the Bible can greatly assist you in your Christian walk. **The following paragraphs in this book are specially designed enable you to achieve this.** Of significant importance to the messengers of this book is the question of family happiness. **This aspect of your new walk as a Christian will be explored in the following paragraphs.**

FACTORS TO CONSIDER WHEN YOU HAVE ACCEPTED CHRIST

There are some **important factors to consider when you have accepted Christ.** Your life will be supernaturally changed. You will become empowered as you walk in obedience to Him. **From henceforth the Holy Spirit would guide and influence your speech and actions.** I have every confidence that this book will bring to you a new light, a new illumination, indeed, a new revelation of certain things which previously seemed so perplexing. **These challenges will now be seen in a new light.**

For further enquiries, contact Brother Charles at 1868475-8971 or 1868381-1964 or email me on Skype name **jesusiscomingyou,** or ooVoo, **blessedone5**. I will be very happy to give you any additional information which may assist in fostering an understanding of your new life and role as a Christian. **And now, open these pages and begin enjoying your new remarkable, reliable and readable book.**

N C Charles
Blessed One!

Congratulation, God bless you as you read this marvelous book

Look for these Books In the future;
THEY will Change your life for good, believe me!

(One) Revealing Biblical Gospel to You!

(Two) Understanding God's wisdom and Solutions To Everyday Problems

(Three) Be Free From Pornography

(Four) I Was Judged, and Condemned!

(Five) The Only True Way to Demonstrate Love and its meaning!

(Six) Gay, I Love You Hear This!

(Seven) Enlightening you: The Lies Told by Some Pastors

(Eight) Empowering Women's Life!

(Nine) Revealing the Secrets and Its, Truth about Rock and Roll, Hip-Hop, Rap, Pop, Chutney, Soca and Dancehall

(Ten) The Last Hour and What It Will Be Like!

(Eleven) Some Say, White Men Wrote the Bible, to imprison the Minds of People, is This True?

And much more to come!

CHAPTER 1

What Is True Marriage?

Today they are so many people who misunderstand what marriage really is. I think that marriage is woefully misconstrued in our society. **Even some pastors seem not to have a clear understanding of this institution called marriage.** One of the major characteristics of a Godly marriage is undoubtedly fidelity. **From biblical times even up to this present day, many spouses continue to be unfaithful to each other.** Moreover, most people expect married spouses to be sexually faithful to each other. **This is a very reasonable expectation and with this you must agree.** This view of marital fidelity agrees with the Bible.

The Scripture says: "**Marriage is honorable in all and the bed undefiled, but whoremongers and adulterers God will judge.**" (Romans 3:4) This scripture verse clearly shows us the degree to which God has exalted the institution of marriage. **Consequently, marriage must be honored, revered, respected and is not to be entered into frivolously or unadvisably.** One must always be faithful to one's spouse. God has declared that he will punish spouses who are adulterous for the scriptures warns that "whoremongers and adulterers God will judge." (Hebrews 13:4) **My friend, the question is: What is true marriage?**

What Is True Marriage?

"He that hath ears to hear let him hear" (Luke 8:8)

What is true marriage? **Some say it is just a tradition. Others: it is just a front, or cover-up for evil doings. Some even marry for citizenship.** Today, marriage is simply seen as a legal document, thus, you may ask the question: Is there a **true marriage? What does the Bible say or teach about it? There are professional marriage counselors** who usually advise couples that are attempting to find solutions to problems within their marriage.

Sadly though, many of their solutions lead to divorce or separation. And that is wrong! Sometimes, it is good to run from problems, but this one is different. Why? You will learn the answer in minutes. **Nevertheless he who instituted marriage has also made a manual (the Bible) to troubleshoot; that is, to identify marital problems and provide the Godly solutions.** Biblical view of marriage: **My friend, allow the word of God be your marriage guide and counselor.** Jude 1:25 describes Jesus as the only wise God and this is evidenced by the biblical solutions which he gives to the range of marital issues which beset mankind.

Today, I observe that the sanctity of marriage, which was once so highly esteemed, has sadly and significantly deteriorated. How has this foundational pillar of civilization crumbled? **My friend, reject ungodly counsel. Marriage is a covenant relationship.** Today marriage counselors even advise married persons to leave each other despite the fact that Jesus have said, "What therefore God hath joined together, let no man put asunder." (Matthew 19:6) **One pastor told a woman: "If your husband doesn't give you money, leave him; he is a foolish man, he cannot give you anything.** So, you go find a man who can help you financially and who really loves and cares for you."

Is this right? What does God have to say about this pastor's statement? I believe this is what the pastor should have said to the woman: **"Help your husband, and have faith in God. His word says: 'Wives, submit yourselves unto your own husbands!'** Jesus never approved that a Christian should divorce his or her spouse. **Marriage means, whole-hearted** commitment and loyalty to one another until death. Now, when you are married you can no longer think as a single person.

The pastor saw two, but God saw one! "For the LORD God of Israel saith that he hateth putting away" (divorce) (Malachi 3:160 "Therefore, what God has joined together, let not man put asunder." Let not the wife depart from her husband. But and if she departs, let her remain unmarried or be reconciled to her husband. And let not the husband put away his wife." (1Corintians7:10-11) My friend, is a marriage now just talk? Has it now degenerated into something meaningless to such a significant number of people? I'm sorry, but I do not think it's something meaningless! True marriages are presided over by the Omnipotent, the Most High, Himself where He joins and unites two hearts together as one.

As a result of the input of God, He has declared "What therefore God has joined together let no man put asunder." (Matthew 19:6) It would indeed be very foolhardy for anyone to trifle with what God has joined together. Therefore, when marriage vows are sacredly and scrupulously kept by both spouses I guarantee you that there will be no problems of infidelity in that marriage. Even this serves as a testimony of the two hearts which God has indeed united together as one. Indeed, marriage is that union in which God unites two persons which become one. Commitment and faithfulness should be imperatives in every marriage, and God should be the head and given pre-eminence.

We know people marry for different reasons, such as money, beauty, job positions, and even religion etc. **These scenarios can lead to so many problems, because in each case, the two individuals were married for selfish gain. In the end, they will be sorry, for when individuals become married for selfish gain, this could lead to sin.** They will have affairs with other persons, because in the first place their hearts were not united together in marriage. **As I said earlier, true marriage is when the two hearts are united together as one (this is the legal).** Love will be forever an everlasting bliss.

Very Important Explanation!

God does the joining. Commitment from the heart is a prerequisite for a successful marriage. **In other words, true marriage occurs when two hearts are joined together by God and are united as one.** This bond that is thus formed then serves as the basis or foundation on which a successful and happy marriage is built. **'Legal' means having God's approval. Marriages are enhanced and taken to a higher level when God unites the two hearts into becoming one.** Indeed, two persons can be married, but if that essential commodity called love is missing, there will eventually be a lack of harmony and fellowship in that relationship. **As I said legal means God's approval of that marriage.**

Now, if one should marry without understanding the true significance of marriage, one may seek exit routes that are not really there. Let me explain. If we say that **marriage involves two hearts being joined together and united by God, then true commitment will certainly enhance that relationship. Then, my question to you is this:** If two persons don't really love each other from the heart and they eventually become married, **then, sometime afterwards one of the spouses may want a divorce because he or she, has found someone else they truly love. As I said legal means God's approval of that marriage.**

Then my question to you is this. Can he or she marry that new-found lover? **Now, you may say that they are "simply" married, according to the law, and since they did not really and truly love each other from the heart, theirs was not a true marriage and as a result, he or she can then be married to another person and not be guilty of the sin of adultery.** My friend, that will be a gross misunderstanding of the tenets of the marriage Covenant. If it were so, I would have told you. **Allow me the privilege of addressing some of those difficult questions and perplexing issues which affect marriages today.**

For example, **one of your family members makes a will leaving 20 acres of land for you, which can only be accessed when they die. You have no choice but to wait until that time to make your claim.** What I'm saying to you is: the only way you can remarried, is if your spouse dies. You may ask, Why? You will learn the reason in chapter 4. **Marriage is a contract. If a man and a woman becomes married and don't love each other, they are still obligated to fulfill the demands of the contract.** You are bound by the law to each other for as long as you are alive. **But if one of you dies, the contract is broken and the surviving partner is free to remarry. There is no way out except one after one of the spouses has died.** (Romans 7:2-3)

I will explain the history of marriage in the next chapter.

CHAPTER 2

What is the History of Marriage?

The history of marriage is misunderstood, (miscalculated) but I will explain some of the marriages to prove a point. Jewish matrimonial tradition was similar to the example given in that illustration. **Today, millions of Christians (and some Non-Christians) say that the only ground for divorce is unfaithfulness and that the individual who wasn't unfaithful could divorce and remarry again.** First I will discourse the history of the Jewish marriage, and the marriage of the church afterwards. **In a Jewish marriage, the only ground on which the Jewish man could have divorced his wife was for fornication. If she committed adultery, she could have been stoned to death.**

(Deuteronomy 22:22) **I will elaborate on this in the subsequent chapters.** My friend please note that this divorce amendment in the book of Matthew 19:9 "except it be for fornication" was annexed to the Law of Moses and it was never given to the church nor to the Gentiles. **Even if it was, it never said that one could be remarried after divorce. It is also stated that "whoso marrieth her which is put away doth commit adultery."** Suffice it to say for the time being, that that divorce amendment before Matthew 19:9 was never given to the church nor to the Gentiles. Your explanation is now forthcoming. My friend, we are told in the book of Malachi 2:16 'The Lord the God of Israel saith that he hateth putting away.' (Divorce)

This bit of scripture informs us of precisely of God's sentiments toward divorce. And to re-enforce this, He commands us in 1 Corinthians 7:10-11 **"And unto the married I command, yet not I, but the LORD, let not the wife depart from her husband, but and if she depart, let her remain unmarried or be reconciled to her husband . . ."** If you are divorced, remember you cannot remarry whilst your husband is alive. (Romans 7:2-3) **Therefore, what if you are married and subsequently realize that your spouse is a person who drinks, smokes, flirts, steals and tell lies?** Or worse, if your spouse turns out to be a drunkard or drug addict, and is also indulging in extra marital sexual relationships? Well, **it now becomes clear to you that this is the person with whom you have decided to spend the balance of your earthly life. It**

suddenly dawns upon you that your spouse have been deceptive and unfaithful. **This is not what you expected!** So now you want a divorce.

What does the bible say? The book of Malachi 2:16 states that the Lord, the God of Israel saith that he hateth putting away (divorce). **My friend, his sentiments, in respect to divorce has not changed.** Neither will he change the word which has already gone out of his mouth. It remains the same for us today, **"For I am the Lord I change not."** (Malachi 3:6) But my friend, there is still hope. **"The Characteristics of a Good Woman and Immoral Woman"** is a book, for you. You can avoid such traumatic situations if you will only take heed and obey what the gospel teaches: **"Be ye not unevenly yolked together with unbelievers."** (2 Corinthians 6:14)

As you saw in the previous verses, the Law of Moses administered over the Jewish matrimonial custom with the death penalty in force for adultery. We all are aware of the fact that a married non Jewish or Gentile woman/wife **can commit adultery. Jesus knew this. That is why he used the Greek word moikia for adultery and the Greek word pornia for fornication in.** (Matthew 19:9) The Jewish matrimonial tradition is different from what obtains in other jurisdictions of the world. **When a Jewish male is espoused (engaged) to a Jewish maiden (young girl) he enters into a covenant and pays a price for her.**

A condition of that covenant (agreement) is that she must be a virgin. Now, if on the wedding night when the marriage is being consummated she is found not to be a virgin, the Law of Moses commands that she should be stoned to death. (Leviticus 20:10) **However, Jesus the true law giver (James4:12) instructed the Jewish men that they should no longer stone her to death but could now put her away (divorce).** Also, read John 8:3-11, **where Jesus' intervention stopped the execution of the Jewish woman caught in the act of adultery.** Now, turn your attention to the wife mentioned in Deuteronomy 24:4. **What does the bible tell us?**

It tells us this: after her first husband had divorced her and sent her out of his house she may become another man's wife. After which she becomes defiled. What is that! Deuteronomy 24:4 **explains.** When a Jewish husband had divorced his wife and after she becomes another man's wife she is now defiled. **Similarly, if a Jewish man's wife was found to have had premarital sex (fornication) he was now allowed to put her away instead of stoning her to death as was commanded by the Law of Moses.** My dear friend this is the reason why you would see the "except for fornication" in the book of Matthew. **You will see it nowhere else in the entire bible.**

Matthew was addressing that peculiar Jewish matrimonial custom, whereas Mark's discourse which targeted the Romans, (Gentiles) has no, "except for fornication" clause. Mark 10:11 says: **"Whosoever shall**

put away his wife, and marry another comitteth adultery against her. And if a woman shall put away her husband and be married to another, she committeth adultery. Similarly, when Luke addresses the entire Gentile world there is also no except for fornication-clause. Luke 16:18 says "**Whosoever putteth away his wife, and marrieth another, comitteth adultery: and whosoever marrieth her that is put away from her husband comitteth adultery.**"

No, except for fornication clause, but for the Jews recorded in the book of Matthew 19:9. Now you have the evidence, my friend. Therefore, you can plainly see why the Jewish husband could have put away (divorced) his wife. Please notice that this judgment was not given to any nation, other than the children of Israel, by Moses, their lawgiver. (John7:19) My friend, I am absolutely certain that this divorce amendment is specific to the Jewish Nation of Israel and I am certain that you are also. Jesus in that discourse with the scribes and Pharisees recorded in Matthew 19:3-9 was treating with Jewish persons who were under the Law of Moses.

This is evidenced by the fact that they came unto Jesus tempting him, saying unto him, is it lawful for a man to put away his wife for every cause? They were specifically expressing what the Law of Moses stated in the book of Deuteronomy 24:1; additional proof that those Pharisees were referring to the Law of Moses. Matthew 19:7. Quoted here for ease of reference "Why did Moses then command to give a writing of divorcement, and to put her away."? These Jewish men were simply repeating what Moses had written in the law. **My friend, this is what the Law of Moses stated in** Deuteronomy 24:1 **"let him give her a bill of divorcement, and give it in her hands and send her out of his house."**

Conclusion: I am sure that this statute was given to no other Nation than the Jews (Children of Israel) because of the fact that the apostle Paul who is also Jewish informs the international community that the Gentiles (ie, non-Jews) do not have the Law of Moses. (See Romans 2:14). **Furthermore, David, a Jewish prophet and descendant of the tribe of Judah also corroborates Paul's testimony in the Book of Psalms 147:19-20** which states: "He showed his word unto Jacob, his statutes and his judgments unto Israel. He had not dealt so with any Nation: and as for his judgments, they have not known them. Furthermore, Amos an Jewish prophet informs us likewise: "O children of Israel" you only have I known of all the families of the earth (Amos 3:2)

My friend we have here overwhelming evidence given and corroborated by three credible Jewish prophets, that the law of Moses was given to no other nation other than the Jewish nation (the children of Israel). Why not believe them. Jesus said in the book of Luke 24:25 **"O fools and slow of heart to believe all that the prophets had spoken."** Hence the reason I am absolutely sure that Non-Jewish persons (Gentiles) and nations which do not have the Law of Moses, cannot adopt those Jewish statutes and judgments unto themselves.

My dear friend, as you are about to close this discourse do remember if you are not a Jew, you are a Gentile and therefore you are excluded and even alienated from those peculiar Jewish covenants. **The apostle Paul puts it this way informing us that we were thus alienated when he states in the book of Ephesians that the Gentiles were "aliens and strangers from the commonwealth of Israel."** Ephesians 1: 11-12. My dear friend, there is an overwhelming abundance of evidence which clearly shows that it is not only injudicious but somewhat naïve for a Gentile to seek to be a participant in something from which he has been physically, legally, spiritually and scripturally excluded.

We Cannot Divorce out Spouses!

There is an abundance of evidence which informs us that we cannot divorce our spouses. **But and if we do we must remain unmarried, or be reconciled to our spouses.** My dear friend, I know that we have been told that it was okay for us to put away (divorce) our spouses but from the overwhelming abundance given above we now know that we cannot. **The only reason divorce was permitted under the Jewish matrimonial custom was for fornication by a Jewish wife. (**Matthew19:9**) So, my friend, do remember that we are not under the Law of Moses, but Christ whose house are we. (**Hebrews 3:6**) Before** getting married, get the book called, **"The Characteristics of a Good Woman and Immoral Woman."**

My humble conclusion is this. Moses allowed the Jewish man to put away (divorce) his wife for fornication, and this was in keeping with some of the peculiar statutes and judgements which were given to that Jewish Nation. These are just a few examples. Similarly, **Moses instructed the Jewish father and mother that a disobedient son who was a drunkard and rebellious should be executed by being stoned to death.** Deuteronomy 21:18-21. Friend, my question to you is this: **Can we also adopt that Jewish tradition? No, no! I am sorry, we cannot.** I feel constrained to offer one final bit of evidence to support this position.

The Book of Deuteronomy which instructs the Jewish parents to execute their rebellious and drunkard son, also instructed the Israeli man to give his wife a writing of divorcement and to put her out of the house. **Finally we read also in the same** Book of Deuteronomy 22:22: **If a man be found lying with a woman married to a husband, then they shall both of them die.** From this text, Moses has clearly mandated the death penalty for marital infidelity (fornication) and not divorce. **Therefore it is in this context that this question was posed to Jesus: 'Is it lawful for a man to put away his wife for every cause?' That was the normal practice of the Jews; divorcing their wives for every frivolous reason.**

Jesus intervened and put an end to this discriminating practice against the Jewish wife by her Jewish spouse informing the Jewish Nation that they ought no longer to exact the death penalty of fornicating Jewish wives but they could now be divorced instead of being executed. **Letting all Israel know that fornication was the only grounds on which divorce for the Jewish male could be obtained and not any frivolous reasons as was previously practised** Deuteronomy 24:1. For additional proof of this please read the account of the woman taken in the very act of adultery and the readiness of the Scribes and Pharisees to execute her by stoning when Jesus' intervention saved her.

These peculiar statutes and judgements were given only to the nation of Israel. **Therefore, as we come to the conclusion of the issue of fornication,** Matthew 19:9 **it is clear that Jesus was addressing a peculiar Jewish custom.** Now if this peculiar custom given by Moses to the Jewish nation is adopted by other nations, can you see the devastatingly disastrous impact it would have on family life? **Please remember we are not Jews and therefore cannot do those things which Moses commanded the Jews to do.** There were some peculiar circumstances relating to the divorced Jewish wife described in Deuteronomy 24:1.

Moses in that said discourse described this divorced Jewish wife as defiled and an abomination after she was remarried. He further stated that this caused the land to be defiled. The prophet, Jeremiah uttered similar sentiments.

Jeremiah 3:1. **If such was the case of the divorced Jewish wife, why should anyone adopt such a device which Moses declares, leads to calamities of monumental proportions?** Is it strange that this divorced Jewish woman should be called an abomination? Yes, to the other nations of the world, but not to the nation of Israel. Friend you may ask, why? **Here is your answer: Every Jewish person knew that it is only upon the death of a Jewess' husband that she could be remarried.**

Although she may remarry, the Law of Moses specifies the conditions. The book of Deuteronomy is very informative in this regard. Deuteronomy 25:5 commands the Jewish male that if brethren dwell together in harmony and if one of them dies, then one of his brothers should marry his wife and raise up children for his deceased brother. **Friend, please notice the condition which must precede her remarriage. Her husband must be dead.** We also read in the book of Genesis 38:9 we see a second example. Judah's firstborn son, Er, was slain by the Lord and Judah told Onan, his second son, to marry Tamar, Er's wife, and raise up sons for his deceased brother, Er. Onan then went into his brother's wife, but he spilled the seed on the ground, and this thing displeased the Lord and the Lord slew him.

The point here is that her husband has to be dead if she is ever to be remarried. A point worthy of noting is that she should not killed him nor have him murdered. In order to explain this peculiar situation, we turn to Romans 7:2-3: For the woman which hath an husband is bound to the husband as long as he liveth. So you know that women have certain characteristics. A wise man will enquire of these things prior to becoming engaged. **The bible is the perfect book that gives us gives us a heavenly model of how a woman should be. My advice:** *Ask God to send the right woman for you! And to confirm it, get the book called: The Characteristics of a Good Woman and Immoral Woman.*

**The marriage vow is 'till death do us are part'!**

CHAPTER 3

God's Statement and Advice

Marriage in the sight of God is "fixed." For he stated that, "it is not good that the man should be alone." (Genesis 2:18) **The word "helper" used to describe Eve in** Genesis 2:20 **means "to surround, to protect and help." Eve was created to be alongside Adam as his "other half," to be his aid and his helper.** When a man and woman marry, they become "one flesh." **This oneness is manifested most fully in the physical union of sexual intimacy.** The New Testament adds a warning regarding this oneness. **So they are no longer two, but one!** "Therefore what God has joined together, let man put asunder."

Does A Wife Have To Submit To Her Husband?

Nevertheless, let every one of you in particular so love his wife even as himself; and the wife see that she reverence her husband. (Ephesians 5:33) When a woman submits to her husband, she is actually submitting to the Lord. It is an act of worship and love for her Savior, not as that of a weak slave. **Husbands, if you don't love your wife like you should, she will feel insecure.** An insecure woman will try to control and dominate the marriage. This is an instinctive reaction on her part. **So love her, care for her, show her your love and support. This is true marriage. It is the uniting of two hearts together as one, and it must come from the heart.**

The Bible words: **"Wives, submit yourselves unto your own husbands, as unto the Lord.** For the husband is the head of the wife, even as Christ is the head of the church: and he is the savior of the body. **Therefore, as the church is subject unto Christ, so let the wives be to their own husbands in everything.** Husbands love your wives, even as Christ also loved the church, and gave himself for it; that he might sanctify and cleanse it with the washing of water by the word. That he might present it to himself a glorious church, not having spot, or wrinkle, or any such thing; but that it should be holy and without blemish. **So ought men to love their wife as their own body. He that loveth his wife, loveth himself.** For no man ever yet hated his own flesh; but nourisheth and cherished it, even as the Lord does the church (Ephesians 5:22-29).

My friend, submission is a very important issue in relation to marriage. Even before sin entered the world, there was still the principle of headship (1 Timothy 2:13) Adam was created first, and Eve was created to be a "helper" for Adam. (Genesis 2:18-20) **At the same time, since there was no sin, there was no authority for man to obey except God's authority.** When Adam and Eve disobeyed God, sin entered the heart (world) and then authority was needed. Therefore, God established the authority needed to enforce the laws of the land and also to provide us with the protection we need. **First, you need to submit to God, which is the only way you can truly obey Him.** (James 4:7)

In 1 Corinthians 11:2-3, we find that the husband is to submit to Christ as Christ did to God. **Then the verse says that the wife should follow this example and submit to her husband.** My friend, **submission is a natural response to loving leadership, W**hen a husband loves his wife as Christ loves the church (Ephesians 5:25-33), then submission is a natural response from a wife to her husband. **The Greek word translated submit, "hupotasso", is the continuing form of the verb. This means that submission to God or to the government is not a one-time act.** It is a continual attitude, which becomes a pattern of behavior. **The submission talked**

about in Ephesians 5 **is not a one-sided subjection of a believer to a selfish, domineering person.**

Biblical submission is designed to be between two Spirit-filled believers who are mutually yielded to each other and to God. **Submission is a two-way street. Submission is a position of honor and completeness.** When a wife is loved as the church is loved by Christ, submission is not difficult. Ephesians 5:24 says, **"Now as the church submits to Christ, so also wives should submit to their husbands in everything."** This verse is saying that the wife is to submit to her husband in everything that is right and lawful. **Therefore, the wife is under no obligation to obey the husband, if he is telling her to disobey God's law in the name of submission.**

Woman was taken out of Adam's side. **She was not taken out of his head to rule over him, nor out of his feet to be trampled upon by him, but out of his side to be a help to him, under his arm to be protected, and near his heart to be loved.** Please submit to one another out of reverence for Christ. (Ephesians 5:21) In context, everything in Ephesians 5:19-33 is a result of being filled with the Spirit. Spirit-filled believers are to be worshipful (5:19), thankful (5:20), and submissive (5:21). Here, Paul applies the Spirit-filled living principles to husbands and wives in verses 22-33.

Wife, submit to your husband's authority, not because you are inferior, but because this is how God designed the

marital relationship to function. Submission isn't being a "doormat" for her husband. Rather, with the help of the Holy Spirit, a wife submits to her husband, and a husband sacrificially loves his wife. **Husband, love your wife, just as Christ loved the church and gave him-self up for her.** (Ephesians 5:25) **"In this same way, husbands ought to love their wives as their own bodies. He that loveth his wife loveth himself. For no man ever hated his own body, but he nourisheth and cherisheth it, even as the Lord the church.** For this reason a man will leave his father and mother and be united to his wife, and the two will become one flesh." (Ephesians 5:28-31)

When the believing husband and wife institute God's principles, a biblical marriage results. A biblically based marriage is one that is balanced, with Christ as the head of both the husband and the wife. The biblical concept of marriage is a union between two individuals that pictures the oneness of Christ with His church. **So understand: everything begins at the heart: obedience, love, submission, not by word, but by action!**

CHAPTER 4

Marriage Is a Covenant. That's Why It Should Come From the Heart!

My friend, the Scriptures is designed to make your marriage successful. Just follow the principles therein. **Wife, submit to your husband as to the Lord.** For your husband is your head, as Christ is the head of the church, of which he is the Savior of the body. **The first step is.** (Ephesians 5:22-23) **The word "covenant" is defined as "a contract" which is an agreement between two or more parties.** Regardless of the circumstances, God's point of view and the marriage covenant should not be abrogated. (Joshua 9:13-21; 10:1-14) **Marriage is a covenant!** (Malachi 2:14; Proverbs 2:17) **For example, when two virgins are married, and they have intercourse (sex), do you know what happens**

between them? Yes, blood and this is when the covenant between two individuals comes to life.

No Longer Two But One-Even Until Death

My friend, examine the covenant between our Lord Jesus Christ and His church (1 Corinthians 11:17-34; Jeremiah 31:31-34; Hebrews 8:9-13; 10:22-25). The Bible is a covenant book, marriage is a covenant vow. **A woman is bound by the law to her husband as long as he is alive. But if he dies, then his legal claim over her disappears.** This means that, if she should give herself to another man while her husband is alive, she incurs the stigma of adultery. **But if, after her husband's passing she does exactly the same thing, no one could call her and adulterer, or an unfaithful person, for the legal hold over her has been dissolved by her husband's death.**

My friend, the death of Christ on the cross had made you, "dead" to the claims of the Law, and you are free to give yourself in marriage, so to speak, to another, the one who was raised from the death, that you may be productive for God. **"While we were "in the flesh" the Law stimulated our sinful passions and so worked in our nature that we became productive for death!** But now that we stand clear of the Law, the claims which existed are dissolved by our "death", and we are free to serve God not in the old obedience to the letter of the law, **but in a new way, in the spirit." The only Scripture in the**

Bible where you actually find the word 'covenant' used in direct relationship to marriage is at the closing of the former testament.

In response to man's cry as to why the Lord will not accept his weeping and tears, the prophet says, **"Because the Lord has been a witness between you and the wife of your youth, against whom you have dealt treacherously, though she is your companion and your wife by covenant."** (Malachi 2:14) **So, is marriage a covenant? Yes! It is a covenant and much more.** The biblical marriage is a divine picture of Christ and His Bride. In addition to that, the Biblical marriage speaks to us of the mystery of Deity. **In the marriage, the wife can be likened to the Holy Spirit, and the man to the Word of God. It takes both to produce life.** But let's leave the mystical to the side for now. **God considers marriage to be a covenant relationship. Furthermore, marriage is a God-sealed Covenant, for in** (Mark 10:8-9)

Jesus teaches that God Himself joins the husband and the wife together. In Proverbs there are references which appear to relate to the covenant of marriage, Solomon wrote: **"Wisdom will enter your heart, and knowledge will be pleasant to your soul.** Discretion will guard you. Understanding will watch over you, to deliver you from the way of evil, from the man who speaks perverse things; from those who leave the paths of uprightness, to walk in the ways of darkness, **who delight in doing evil, and rejoice in the perversity of evil, whose paths**

are crooked, and who are devious in their ways, to deliver you from the strange woman, from the adulteress who flatters with her words that leaves the companion of her youth, and forgets the covenant (beriyth) of her God. (Proverbs 2:10-17)

All I am saying is that marriage begins in the heart. If you think this is not true, please email me at truthofsalvation463@ymail.com

Making marriage Last-What Is the Key?

My friend, the key to a successful marriage, through the Bible's revelation is that marriage is a covenant. Basically, this means two things: **first of all, it means commitment.** There is no covenant without commitment from the heart. **Marriage is not an experiment, it begins with a commitment. Those who bypass commitment cannot find God's purpose for marriage.** Secondly, in a covenant God sets the terms. He does not leave it to man to decide on what basis a marriage will be ordered. He has laid down certain specific and simple terms.

Another key of marriage is forgiveness. The way to start the healing process in marriage is by confessing your wrong and then asking for forgiveness. (Matthew 6:14-15) Ask for forgiveness as this engenders a sense of empathy and confidence which create the atmosphere for reconciliation. You may both make mistakes occasionally. **You need to be able to forgive, forget, and move on with the relationship.** Marriage is heart and commitments, not just talk, so if you are going and get married, make sure you love the person whom you are marrying **(I am not talking about infatuation but whole-heartedness). Marriage is a covenant**, because if you don't love from your heart, you will have big problems.

Do you want that? Then love from your heart. **The hearts must be united together as one in marriage.** Why? If someone thinks when he is baptized, he will receive the Holy Spirit without believing in his heart, what sense does this make? **Or, if he gets baptized so that he will go to heaven without being changed and without receiving the Spirit of God in his heart, he is fooling himself.** He must be born of the spirit, and renewed in the heart to be saved. Many people say, if I pay my tithes I will get to heaven and receive blessings. This is foolish and thoughtless. **So it is in a marriage; you must also love the Lord with your whole heart. Being united together as one is a true marriage. "Can two walk together, except they be agreed?** (Amos 3:3)

What can the married couple do to ensure that their marriage will last? The first and most important issue is one of obedience to God and His Word. **This is a principle that should be in force before the marriage.** God says, in the Book of Amos "Can two walk together except they be agreed." (Amos 3:3) **Another principle that would protect the longevity of a marriage is along the same line: the husband should obey God and love Him, honoring, and protecting his wife as he**

would his own body (Ephesians 5:25-31) The corresponding principle is that the wife should obey God and submit to her own husband "as to the Lord" (Ephesians 5:22) **The marriage between a man and a woman is a reflection of the relationship between Christ and the church.** Christ gave Himself for the church and he loves, honors, and protects her as his "bride" (Revelation 19:7-9)

My Advice for You to Follow!

Honesty, humility and respect! Being able to say "I'm sorry", "I'm wrong" and mean it. **Listen to each other, every day. Hold hands whether you've been married for 1, 5, 10, or 60 years. Show your wife or husband love always.** My friend, never blame others for your marriage problems Take responsibility and w**ork them out together. Communicate and trust, and lots of love.** That's God's key. And after many years of marriage you will still feel like newlyweds. **Love will endure many things and you will always come out victorious.** Communication and Trust, is the key to making a strong marriage. **Being faithful and show support throughout hard times and good times. And always remember that it takes two to make a relationship last. One love!**

CHAPTER 5

What Is Marital Fidelity?

What is marital fidelity? **Marital fidelity is wholesome faithfulness within a marriage. Marital infidelity is therefore adultery or unfaithfulness within a marriage.** The facts about marital infidelity (sexual unfaithfulness to a spouse) are astounding. With all the talk of infidelity in the press, one might just wonder: What is really marital fidelity? **Here, we will discuss the answer to that question looking at the factual, emotional and physical definitions, and the contributors that are the catalysts to faithfulness or unfaithfulness in marriage.**

1 Dictionary Definition

According to Dictionary.com, the definition of fidelity includes "strict observance of promises, duties, etc." Merriam-Webster's online dictionary says it this way: "the quality or state of being faithful."

2 Roots of Marital Fidelity

Marital fidelity, faithfulness and loyalty to your spouse are rooted in marriage vows. **People don't pledge their unfaithfulness. Instead they profess their faithfulness to one another.** That means that no other person will turn your head or tempt you in the way that your spouse does.

3 Physical Fidelity

To be faithful or loyal to your spouse means that you will save sexual intimacy for your spouse only. You will not allow another person to touch you in a sexual or intimate manner, nor will you touch another person besides your spouse in this way.

4 Emotional Fidelity

Marital fidelity also includes your emotions. You should not share intimate secrets with a person of the opposite sex other than your spouse. Marital fidelity means resisting the temptation to get that close to someone else and reserving those conversations for your husband or wife only. If love is in your heart, you will be guarded.

5 The Second Glance

Have you ever done a double take as an attractive man or woman walks by? Have you ever been tempted by porn? Marital fidelity includes treasuring your spouse so much that you refuse to cheapen it by using outside options to find pleasure. **Please keep away from such!**

Warning Lesson!

My friend, **refrain from sex with other partners. Is that the full extent of what it means to be faithful in marriage?** What about sexual fantasies involving someone or a close friendship with someone of the opposite sex? Is this a form of infidelity? **Are sexual fantasies harmless? The Bible presents sex as a natural and wholesome part of married life, a source of mutual joy and satisfaction.** The Bible says: **"Be happy with the wife you married when you were young. She is beautiful and graceful, just like a deer; you should be attracted to her and stay deeply in love at all times."** (Proverbs 5:18-19)

Today many modern experts believe that it is normal and healthy, and earthly thinking for a married person to fantasize about other sexual partners. **Are such fantasies harmless as long as they are not acted upon?** Do you not feel guilty, if you have sexual fantasies about other persons? **Sexual fantasies typically focus on personal gratification. Such self-centered behavior is contrary to the Bible's advice for married people.** Regarding sexual relation, God says: **"The wife is not the master of her own body, but her husband is; in the same way a husband is not the master of his own body, but his wife is."** (1 Corinthians 7:4)

My friend, consider the Bible principles; it prevents sex from becoming a fantasy fueled by acts of lust and selfishness. **As a result, marriage makes happiness greater enjoyment. This simply means to care about your wife just as you care about yourself.** (Philippians 2:4; Acts 20:35) Fantasies of sex outside of marriage involve mentally rehearsing actions, that if carried out, would cause great emotional pain to one's mate, and engaging in sexual fantasies would increase the likelihood of committing adultery. The Bible illustrates the link between thoughts and actions: **"But a person is tempted by his own desires that drag him off and trap him. His desires make him sin, and when sin is finished with him, it leaves him dead."**

This means his evil desires conceive and give birth to sin, and when it is full-grown, give birth to death. (James 1:14-15) Jesus Christ said: **"I say unto you, That whosoever looketh** on a woman to lust after her hath committed adultery with her already in his heart." This means fantasizing about other sexual partners is wrong. **People, who say such fantasizing is normal and healthy, and natural for a married person to engage in, are so unwise!** My friend, if you look at another woman and want her, you are already unfaithful in your thoughts. (Matthew 5:28) **My friend be careful! Guard your thoughts and your actions because they are the source of true life.** Never tell lies or be deceitful in what you say. **Keep looking straight ahead without turning aside, and you will stay on solid ground.** Don't make a mistake by turning to the right or the left. (Proverbs 4:23-27)

Remain Emotionally Faithful?

My friend, a successful marriage requires; giving "passionate love" to your mate (Song of Solomon 8:6). **Be faithful to your own wife and give your love to her alone.** So be satisfied with your own wife and find complete joy with the girl you married. **My friend: you should be faithful to your wife or husband just as you take water from your own well. Don't be like a stream from which just any woman may take a drink.** Save yourself for your wife and don't have sex with other women. **Be happy with the wife you married when you were young** (Proverbs 5: 15-18). **What does this mean?** Is it normal to have friends of both sexes outside of marriage? Your marriage mate must have the first claim of your time, attention, and emotional energy. **Any relationship that takes what rightly** belongs to your mate and gives it to someone else is a form of "infidelity," even if no sexual activity is involved.

My Friend How Could Such a Relationship Develop?

Today most people don't understand how to develop their own relationships. This results in the disillusion of many relationships. **Someone of the opposite sex may seem more attractive or empathetic than your spouse.** Spending time with that person in the business or workplace can lead to discussing personal matters, including problems or disappointments in your marriage. **An emotional dependency can grow. Communication with the person by telephone or through online chat could become a betrayal of trust. Please avoid this at all costs!**

Marriage mates properly expect that certain topics will be discussed only with each other and that their confidential talk will be kept private. (Proverbs 25:9) **Beware of rationalizing on romantic feelings when in fact they may exist!** The heart is treacherous; says Jeremiah 17:9. **If you have a close friendship with someone of the opposite sex, ask yourself: am I defensive or secretive about the relationship?** Would I be comfortable if my mate overheard our conversations? How would I feel if my mate cultivated a similar friendship? Matthew 7:12 said: **"Treat others as you want them to treat you. This is what the Law of the Prophets is all about."**

Keep away from such people whose intention is to destroy your relationship.

An improper relationship can lead to marital disaster, since emotional closeness paves the way for eventual sexual intimacy. **As Jesus warned; out of the heart comes, evil ideas which leads to murder, unfaithfulness in marriage, vulgar deeds, stealing, telling lies, and insulting others.** (Matthew 15:19). **However, if adultery does not damage the marriage then it will encourage loss of trust which can be extremely difficult to repair.** For example, Shanice, a wife said: **"When I discovered that Mark was secretly talking on the phone several times a day with another woman, my heart was broken.** I wanted to believe that they were not sexually involved. But, it was very hard not to. I was not sure that I could ever trust him again." **Keep friendships with members of the opposite sex within appropriate boundaries.**

Do not ignore the presence of improper feelings or rationalize impure motives. Counsel: **If you sense that a relationship threatens your marriage, act quickly to limit or end it.** The Bible says: **"Sensible people will see trouble coming and avoid it, but an unthinking person will walk right into it and regret it later."** (Proverbs 22:3) "Everyone that keeps on looking at a woman and wants to have possession of her is guilty of committing adultery with her in his heart." (Matthew 5:28)

Protect Your-Flesh Bond

Our Creator intended that marriage should be the closest relationship between two humans. **God said that the husband and wife "must become one flesh."** (Genesis 2:24) The flesh bond involves more than sexual intimacy. **It includes a close emotional bond, which means her husband, puts his confidence in her, and he will never be poor. As long as she lives, she does him well or good and never harm.** This simply means that her husband depends on her, and she will never let him down. She is good to him every day of her life. (Proverbs 31:11-12) **In the same way, a husband should love his wife as much as he loves himself.** A husband who loves his wife shows that he loves himself. None of us hate our own bodies.

My friend, you should be responsible for your wife, taking good care of her, just as Christ does for the church, because each member is a part of his body. As the Scriptures say, "A man leaves his father and mother to get married, and he becomes like one person with his wife. "In other words one flesh." **This is a great mystery, but I understand it to mean Christ and the church.** So each husband should love his wife as much as he loves himself, and each wife should respect her husband. (Ephesians 5:28-33) **Applying those principles will help to protect your marriage from damage caused by mental and emotional unfaithfulness.** All married couples and those who are planning to get married, read and understand. If your relationship is broken, mend it with the help of God. **Keep these principles close to your heart, and you will overcome all problems. Remember to love unconditionally, one love!**

CHAPTER 6

The Basic Principle to Make Your Family Live Happily!

Today many people don't know how to have family happiness, where to look for it and from where to receive it. Husband, if you are not fulfilling your roles, this may lead to several problems. God wants your family life to be happy, so **He provides guidelines for each family member. God has a role that He wants each member to play.** When family members fulfill their roles in keeping with God's word,(the Bible) harmony ensues. Jesus said: **"Yea rather, blessed are they that hear the word of God, and keep it"** This is true! People who are really blessed are the ones who hear and obey God's messages! (Luke 11:28)

My friend, a family will have conflict within their relationship because, true family happiness depends mainly on recognizing that the Father originates with Jesus Christ; the one Jesus called, "Our Father" (Matthew 6:9) Every family on earth exists because of God the Father and he certainly knows what makes families happy. (Ephesians 3:14-15) **What does the Bible teach about the role of each family member, which, if adhered to, will lead to happiness?** God created the first humans, Adam and Eve, and brought them together as husband and wife. He placed them in a beautiful home called the Garden of Eden and told them to have children. **"Be fruitful, and multiply, and replenish the earth."** (Genesis 1:26-28)

This is not just a fairy tale or a myth. Christ Jesus quoted what Genesis says about the start of family life. It is therefore absolutely true: (Genesis 2:24) **"Therefore a man shall leave his father and mother and be joined to his wife." My friend, you see why it is important to imitate God; this leads to happiness within the family. It is possible, that each member of the family can help to make family life happy by imitating God in showing love and care.** Do as God does! After all, you are his dear children. Let love be your guide! Christ loved us and offered his life for us as a sacrifice that pleased God. (Ephesians 5:1-2; John 1:14-18)

To avoid problems, God, the Father, gives a role to each member of the family: the husband, wife and children.

Playing your role obediently will prevent problems and conflicts. Therefore, by learning about the love that Jesus showed and following his example, each one of you can help to make family life better-off.

A Role for a Husband

Husband, the Bible says that you should treat your wife in the same way that Jesus treats his disciples. Consider this Bible direction: **Continue loving your wife just as Christ also loved the Congregation and delivered up himself for it. In the same way, a husband ought to love his wife as his own body.** He who loves his wife loves himself for no man can ever hate his own. **Husband, do this and your family will live a happy life. Respect one another; do not ill-treat each other.**

Each family member ought to acquaint themselves with the love Jesus showed toward his congregation. This sets forth the perfect example also for the husband. **One of the things that can cause problems within a family is the lack of forgiveness of sins. As I said earlier, the key to happiness is forgiveness. The healing process in marriage commences by confessing your wrong and asking for forgiveness.** (Matthew 6:12; 6:14-15) Ask for forgiveness! Within a marriage, spouses and even children must have a sense of empathy and forgiveness.

You're all going to make mistakes on occasions. **You need to be able to forgive, forget, and move on with the relationship.**

You must forgive others the wrong they have done to you. **Do this and live happily!** Jesus' love for his congregation sets a perfect example for the husband. Jesus loved them so much that he sacrificed his life for them even though they were far from perfect. (John 13:1-15) Likewise husband, keep on loving your wife and do not abuse or be harsh towards her. (Colossians 3:19) **My friend, what will help a husband when his wife commits adultery or fails to act with discretion? He should remember his own mistakes.** He must receive God's forgiveness. What is that? He must forgive those who sin against him, and that includes his wife. Alternatively, she should do the same. (Matthew 6:12-15**)**

    Do you see why some have said that a successful marriage is the union of two good forgivers? Read what God said about a person who commits adultery (Hebrews 13:4) Husband, you must always show consideration for your wife; remember Jesus always showed consideration for his disciples. **He took into account their limitations and physical needs.** For example he said, "Come ye yourselves apart into a desert place, and rest a while." (Mark 6:30-32). **Wives also deserves thoughtful consideration. If you are a husband, you should be thoughtful and have a proper understanding of your wife. Treat her with honor and respect, because she is not as strong as you are, and she shares with you in the gift of life.** Then nothing will interfere or stand in the way of your prayers (Peter 3:7)

Remember that it is faithfulness, which makes one precious to God. It is immaterial whether you are male or female. (Psalm 101:6)

How to Make Your Wife Happy?

My friend, this is just for you and your wife. You are no longer two people, but **one.** God said: **"Wherefore they are no more twain, but one flesh. What therefore they God hath joined together, let not man put asunder."** (Matthew 19:6) Be **faithful to your own wife and give your love to each other alone, just as you take water from your own well.** In addition, do not be like a stream from which just any woman may take a drink. **Save yourself for your wife and do not have sex with other women. Be happy with the wife you married.** (Proverbs 5:15-21) "Marriage is honourable in all, and the bed undefiled: but whoremongers and adulterers God will judge." (Hebrews 13:4).

Husband and wife, be fair to each other about having sex. **Do not refuse sex to each other, unless you have agreed not to have sex for a little while, in order to spend time in prayer.** Then Satan won't be able to tempt you because of your lack of self-control. **Why do not refuse sex?** The Bible will answer you; **"The wife hath not power ((the master) of her own body, but the husband: and likewise also the husband hath not power (the master) of his own body, but the wife."** You, Wife, belong to your husband, and you, Husband belong to your wife. (1 Corinthians 7:4-5) **Noteworthy is the reminder: 'For no man ever yet hated his own flesh; but nourisheth and cherisheth it, even as the Lord the church."** Husband, you need to love your wife as you do yourself, remember that she is accountable to her own head, Jesus Christ (Ephesians 5:29; 1 Corinthians 11:3)

An Example, a Role for a Wife!

A family is an organization. To operate smoothly, it needs a head. Remember: **"that the head of every man is Christ; and the head of the woman is the man; and the head of Christ is God."** (1 Corinthians 11:3). Jesus' submission to God's headship is a fine example. **All of us have a head to whom, we must submit. Imperfect men make mistakes and often fall far short of being ideal family heads. So what should a wife do?** Wife you should not belittle your husband nor try to take over his headship. Wife remembers this always! God view, **a quiet and gentle spirit is of great value and God considers it very great price.** (1 Peter 3:4)

By displaying such a spirit, it is easier to demonstrate Godly subjection even under frustration. What is the example mentioned at Philippians 1:8, and why should a husband display this quality towards his wife? How does Jesus provide an example for wives? **What attitude should a wife have towards her husband and what may be the effect of her conduct?** What does the Bible say? It teaches us: **"The**

wife should reverence her husband." (Ephesians 5:33) **So wife if your husband falls, help him up, don't try to take his headship, for you are his helper, so help him, and you will be a good wife, and God will reward you.**

By so doing, you will have proven that you have that power of a virtuous woman, as the Proverbs 31:12 said: **"She will do him good and not evil all the days of her life." Wife, if your husband falls, let him be able to say, "I can put my confidence in my wife, she will never let me go under, but help me to my feet."** In other words she would help him administer his leadership. (Proverbs 31:10-12) What if he does not accept Christ as his head? The Bible urges wives: "Ye wives, be in subjection to you own husband; that, if any obey not the word, they also may without the word be won by the conversation of the wives." **I promise you, it will not be necessary for you to say a word because they will see how pure and reverent your conduct is.** (1 Peter 3:1-2)

Whether or not her husband is a believer, she would not show her disrespect if she tactfully expresses an opinion that differs from his. **Her viewpoint may be correct and the whole family could benefit if he listens to her. In Genesis 21:9-12 Abraham did not agree when his wife, Sara corrected him. Do you know what God told him? He said: "Hearken unto her voice." When a husband makes a final decision that is not at conflict with God's law, his wife should show her subjection by supporting him.** Read Acts 5:29; Ephesians

5:24 to find the answer. In fulfilling her role, a wife can do much in caring for the family.

A married woman should love her husband and her children. She should be sound in mind, sensible and kind, as well as a good homemaker who puts God first. (Titus 2:4-5) **A wife and mother who acts in that ways will gain the lasting love and respect from her family.** (Proverbs 31:10-29) **The Bible counsels:** "Let not the wife depart from her husband: But and if she depart, **let her remain unmarried or reconciled to her husband:** and let not the **husband put her wife.**" I do not know of anything else the Lord said about marriage." (1 Corinthians 7:10-12)

Perfect Examples for a Parent, And Children

Jesus sets a perfect example for a parent in the way he treated children. When others tried to prevent the little ones from approaching, Jesus said. **"Suffer the little children to come unto me, and forbid then not, for of such is the kingdom of God."** The Bibles also said: **"And he took them up in his arms, put his hands upon them, and blessed them."** (Mark 10:13-16) Since Jesus took time for little ones, parent do you do the same for your own sons and daughters? **They need not small bits of your time but large amounts of it.** You need to take time to teach them for that is what God instructs you to do.

Children, obey your parents who should always tell you what God says, and teach you Bible principles. Anything other than God's word must be rejected. **God made it clear that: "Children, obey your parents in the Lord: for this is right. Honour thy father and mother; which is the first commandment with a promise; that it be well with thee, and thou mayest live long on the earth."** Parents please obey God as well: "And, ye fathers provoke not your children to wrath: but bring them up in the nurture and admonition of the Lord." (Ephesians 6: 1-4)

How did Jesus treat children and what do children need from parents? **As this world becomes ever wicked, children need parents who will protect them from people who seek to harm them, such as sexual predators.** Consider this! As a parent, you need to pay attention to the **Devil's** attempts to harm your little ones. You need to give them advice and warning. Remember the Scripture said: "Be sober, be vigilant; because your adversary the devil, as a roaring lion, walketh about, seeking whom he may devour." (1 Peter 5:8) **Jesus said unto him, "I am the way, the truth and the Life: no man cometh unto the Father, but by me."** (John 14:6).

Parents Learn From the Way Jesus Treated Children

My friend, on the night before Jesus died his disciples argued about who was greater among them. **They became angry with each other.** Jesus lovingly continued to appeal to them by word and example. (Luke 22:24-27; John 13:3-8) If you are a parent, can you see how you might follow Jesus' example in the way he corrected his disciples? **Truly they need discipline but it should be given to the proper degree and never in anger. You would not want to speak thoughtlessly as with the stabs of a sword.** (Jeremiah 30:11)

Proverbs 12:18 said: "There is not speaketh like the piercings of a **sword: but the tongue of the wise is health**" My friend, disciplining should be in such a way that your child will later see how appropriate it was. The Bible says: **Parent do not be hard on your children. Raise them properly.** Teach them and instruct them about the Lord. (Ephesians 6:4; Hebrews 12:9-11) Be a model for your children. Can children learn from Jesus? Yes they can! By his own example Jesus showed how children should obey their parents.

Just as the Father taught me he said: **"I do nothing of myself; but as my Father hath taught me, I speak these things: For I do always those things that please him."** (John 8:28-29) Jesus was obedient to his Heavenly Father and the Bible tells children to obey their parents in the Lord. (Ephesians 6:1-3) Although Jesus was a perfect child, he obeyed his human parents, Joseph and Mary who were imperfect. That surely contributed to the happiness of every member of Jesus' family. (Luke 2:4-5)

The Way That Children Can Make Their Parents Happy

Young ones may sometimes find it difficult to obey their parents, why? **They are being disciplined in the wrong way. Can parents learn from the way that Jesus handled his disciples' imperfections?** In what ways did Jesus set a perfect example for children? Why did Jesus, always obey his Heavenly Father, and who is happy when children obey their parents today? That is what God wants children to do. (Proverbs 1:8; 6: 20-22) **Jesus always obeyed his Father even under difficult circumstances.**

One day, when Jesus had to do God's will, he said "Father, if thou be willing, remove this cup from me: nevertheless not my will, but thine, be done." Jesus did what God asked because he realized that his Father knew well, and he loved his Father, so he obeyed Him. (Luke 22:42) My son and daughter, by learning to be obedient, you will make your parents and the Heavenly Father very happy. (Proverbs 23:22-25) **The Devil tempted Jesus Christ and we can be sure that he will also tempt young ones to do what is evil and wrong.** (Matthew 4:1-10) Satan, the Devil uses peer pressure, which can be difficult to resist. **How vital it is that children do not keep company with wrongdoers!** (1 Corinthians 15:33)

"Be not deceived: evil communication corrupt good manners." Jacob's daughter Dinah kept company with those who did not worship the true God and this led her to a lot of trouble. (Genesis 34:1-3) My son and daughter, **think of how the family could be hurt if one of its members were to become involved in sexual immorality!**(Proverbs 17:21-25) **If a parent asked a child to break God's law would it be right for the child to disobey them. Read** (Acts 5:29) **Yes!** What should young people think about when they are tempted? Give two (2) answers (James 1:12-18)

1 ....

2 ....

What Is the Key to all Family Happiness?

Family problems are easier to cope with when Biblical counsel is applied. In fact, applying such counsel is the key to family happiness. Therefore, husband love your wife and treat her as Jesus treats his church. **Wife, you submit to the headship of your husband and follow the example of the capable wife described at** in Proverbs 31:10-31. Husband, remember to manage your household in a fine manner. (1Timothy 3:4-8) In addition, children you must always obey your parents. (Colossians 3:20)

Father, mother and children, forgive one another for forgiveness is the practice of a successful family. Truly, the

Bible contains a wealth of valuable counsel and instruction regarding family life. The Bible said "And God shall wipe away all tears from their eyes; and there shall be no more death, neither, sorrow, nor crying, neither shall there by any more pain: for the former things are passed away." (Revelation 21:3-4) **What a wonderful home which lies ahead for our families through Christ!** Even now, you can enjoy happy family life by applying God's instructions and principles found in his word, the Bible.

Follow God's principle and your family will be happy; not only happiness, but they all will have a life in heaven. One Love!

CHAPTER 7

Many Pastors Don't Speak With the Authority from God That Influences Men

Most teachers who speak today speak with no authority. That's why many people are still living in sins. **They speak for selfish gain!** However, when Jesus speaks as the only-begotten Son of God and we apply His words in our life **Changes take place immediately. He certainly speaks like no other man because he speaks with authority influencing people, like when he spoke on the Sermon on the Mount!** Read (Matthew 7:28-29). Jesus did not teach as the scribes, who based their worldly speeches on the teachings of imperfect humans, telling men what they want to hear, like some pastors do today. **Christ Jesus taught as a person having authority because what he spoke came from God, the Father.**

Some pastors speak about healing but half of their members are sick or dying; some even have unclean spirits. Others are blind, dumb, lame or crippled. On the other hand some even have cancers and HIV, etc. (Matthew 15:29-31; Luke 9:2) **These pastors cannot do anything for those people because they need Jesus in their lives, to have authority over these sickness.** They are also self-centered, selfish, and are inconsiderate and most of all, proud. So how could they expect to do miracles? **My friend for miracles to take place, you must have humility.** Jesus says "Behold, I give unto you power to tread on serpents and scorpions, and over all the power of the enemy: and nothing shall by any means hurt you." (Luke 10:19; 19:10)

Pastor you need to get your act together. Help the people, and be an asset, not a liability to them. Teacher Jesus said, "I know this commandment is life everlasting; whatsoever I speak therefore, even as the Father said unto me, so I speak." (John 12:50) Let us see how Jesus further sayings in the Sermon on the Mount can and should influence our authority **Jesus said never pray as the hypocrites do. Prayer is an important part of true worship, and you ought to pray to the Most High regularly.** But your prayer should be influenced by Jesus' sayings in the Sermon on the Mount. When you pray do not be like the hypocrites! **They love to stand up and pray in the synagogues (church) and on the street corners, to be visible to men.** My friend, do you see these kinds of things happening?

YOURS TRULY
MESSENGER MR. NICHOLAS C. CHARLES

Yes, **they stand up in the church boasting of their businesses, properties, and of their education, such as degrees, masters, doctorate, etc.** Truly I say to you, they are having their reward in full. (Matthew 6:5) Jesus' disciples were not to imitate such "hypocrites" as the self-righteous Pharisees, whose public display of piety was nothing more than a pretence. **Those hypocrites liked to pray standing in the houses of worship and on the street corners,** why? So they could be visible to men. **For selfish gain!** My friend, **so-called teachers want to be visible to men, so they can be praised, that is why they boast about such thoughtlessness.** (Matthew 23:13-32). They want you to boast as well: "My pastor has Doctorate; he is an educated man!"

Friend, do not be a hypocrites like them. Having a doctorate doesn't give anyone unction to be a pastor. You must be called by God, not education. It's all about showing off. Jesus said: "Which devour widows' houses, and for a shew make long prayers: the same shall receive greater damnation." (Luke 20:47) My Christian brother and sister that is not the attitude that we should have; Jesus Christ declared that such hypocrites were having their reward in full. They greatly desired recognition and praise from fellow humans and that was all they would get. They would not get blessings from God because they did not do it for him. I would not answer their hypocritical prayers, said God.

On the other hand, God would respond to the prayers of Jesus' true followers, by Jesus further statement on this subject. "Thou, when thou prayest, enter into thy closet, and when thou hast shut thy door, pray to thy Father which is in secret, and thy Father which seeth in secret shall reward thee openly." (Matthew 6:6) **My friend, let me make that statement a little clearer. Jesus does not mean you should not pray before a congregation in prayer.** What Jesus is saying, when you are praying, do not say the same things over and over again, just as the people of the nations do when they are praying. Do not use a lot of meaningless words, just to impress others.

In other words when you pray don't talk on and on as people who don't know God. They think God likes to hear long prayers. Don't be like them. Your Father knows what you need before you ask. **(Matthew 6:7-8)** Remember what Jesus said about unacceptable prayers. It should remind us that God is not impressed by high-sounding speech and superfluous (redundant) words. **We should also realize that public prayer is not on occasion to try to impress people or cause them to wonder how long it will be before they say "Amen."** Using prayer to make announcements or to counsel the audience would also be out of harmony with the Spirit **of Jesus as stated in the Sermon on the Mount.**

Today some ministers are so important that they cannot even carry they own Bibles. **Paul said: Don't worry about anything, but pray about everything, with thankful hearts** offer up your prayers and requests to God. Then, because **you belong to Christ Jesus,** God will bless you with peace that no one can completely understand. And this peace will control the way you think and feel. **Church leaders, it is necessary to wake up. God will punish you, for not doing what you have to do. He is so displeased that He can say:** "In vain they do worship me, teaching for doctrines the commandments of men." (Matthew 15:9)

Jesus Teaches Us How to Pray

You may wonder how some pastors, pray so superfluously. (1) Friend, such praying is to impress people (2) **It is for some people to say, "This man could pray, boy, he can pray really pray well. That is not prayer, that is meaningless words, as** Matthew 6:7-8 **describes it.** The Bible said: "When ye pray, use not vain repetitions, as the heathen do: for they think that they shall be heard for their much speaking. Be not ye therefore like unto them: for your Father knoweth what things ye have need of, before ye ask him." Deuteronomy 32:6 said: "Do ye thus requite the LORD, O foolish people and unwise? Is not he thy Father that hath bought thee? Hath he not made thee, and established thee"? (2 Chronicles 6:21; Acts17:24-28)

When we say, **"Thy kingdom come. Thy will be done on earth as it is in heaven,"** what does it mean? (Matthew 6:10) In connection with this prayer request, we should remember that the "Kingdom" is the Heavenly messianic government in the hands of Christ and the resurrected holy ones associated with him, (Daniel 7: 13-18) **Praying for it to "come" is a request that God's kingdom come against all earthly opposition of divine ruler-ship.** That will soon occur in the new heaven and in the new earth, where righteousness and peace will be established at our eternal home.

For example: **At the time of those rules the God of Heaven will establish a kingdom that will never end.** It will never be conquered, but will completely destroy all those empires and then last forever. (2 Peter 3:13; Daniel 2:44) The Father is in heaven, and He is asking that his will take place on earth, including the removal of his enemies. Give us today the food we need. (Matthew 6:11; Luke 11:3) By making this imploring request, we are asking God to provide necessary food "Give us this day our daily bread." **This indicates that we have faith in God's ability to care for our needs on a daily basis. It is not a prayer for surplus provisions.**

This request for our daily needs may remind us that God commanded the Israelites to go out and gather manna each day and gather enough for that day. **Listen to what God said: In this way I can test them and find out if they will follow my instructions. And He will do that to you too.** (Exodus 16: 1-4) This other request captures your attention. Jesus said: **"Forgive us our debts, (the wrongs) as we forgive others debtors." (the wrongs of others)** (Matthew 6:12-15) Jesus said: **"If ye forgive not man their trespasses, neither will your Father**

forgive your trespasses." Instead, be kind and tender-hearted to one another, and forgive one another, as God has forgiven you through Christ. (Matthew 6: 14-15; Ephesians 4:32; Colossians 3:13) "And lead us not into temptation, but deliver us from evil: for thine is the kingdom, and the power and the glory, forever amen." (Matthew 6:13)

How are we to understand those two related requests in Jesus' prayer? One thing is true: God does not tempt us to commit sins. (James 1:13; Matthew 4:3) Satan the wicked one is the real "Tempter." **Therefore, do not bring us into temptation is a petition that God not permit us to succumb when we are tempted to disobey him.** Finally, **"please deliver us from the wicked one,"** is a request that God does not allow Satan to overcome us. And we can be confident that God will not let us be tempted beyond what we can bear. In other words: **Every test that you have experienced is the kind that normally comes to people.**

But God keeps his promise, and he will not allow you to be tested beyond your power to remain firm; at the time you are put to the test, he will give you the strength to endure it, and so provide you with a way out. (1 Corinthians 10:13) My friend: Keep on Asking, Seeking, and Knocking. The apostle, Paul said: Let your hope keep you joyful, be patient in your troubles, and pray at all times. (Romans 12:12) **Jesus shared a powerful point along those lines when he declared: "Ask,**

and it shall be given you: seek, and ye shall find, knock, and it shall be opened unto you:

For every one that asketh receiveth; and he that seekth findeth; and to him that knocketh it shall be opened." (Matthew 7:7-8) It is proper to keep on asking, for anything that is in harmony with God's will. The apostle, John wrote: "And this is the confidence that we have in him, that, if we ask anything according to his will, he heareth us." (1John 5:14) My friend, Jesus encourages us to 'keep on asking and seeking.' We should pray earnestly and not give up at all. He also said it is necessary for us to "keep on knocking" to gain access to the Kingdom and enjoy its blessings, benefits, and rewards. But can we be confident that God will answer our prayers? YES, we can if we are faithful to God.

My friend, "knock and it shall be opened." God is truly the Hearer of Prayer, Psalms 65:2said: "O thou that hearest prayer, unto thee shall all flesh come." Would any of you who are fathers give your son a stone when he asks for bread? Or would you give him a snake when he asks for a fish? As bad as you are, you know how to give good things to your children. How much more then, will your Father in heaven give good things to those who ask him." (Matthew 7: 9-11) A human father although comparatively "Wicked" because of the inheritance of a sinful nature, has natural affection for his offspring. He would not deceive his child but would strive to provide him with **"good gifts."** With a fatherly attitude toward us, our loving Heavenly Father provides us **"good things" such as his Holy Spirit, to those who ask him!"**

Luke 11:13 said: **"If ye then, being evil, know how to give good gifts unto your children: how much more shall your heavenly Father give the Holy Spirit to them that ask him."** (James 1:17)

If you asked God for your healing, open your eyes to the truth. Read this Bible text: Exodus 15: 26, **and see why you are not being healed.**

CHAPTER 8

God is real; Let No One tell you otherwise. He Is the Creator of Heavens and Earth and All Things

Scientists teach that there is no God. Some people believe this error that was designed to deceive the world. **They say that they cannot see God, so there is no God. They go on saying the world made itself. Is this true, my friend? But can I ask you something wonderful.** Who made the flowers? No man did. You're right! But someone made it; it is the Creator, the Heavenly Father of all living things. Yet, someone may say that he believes only what he can see. He may say: if I cannot see, I don't believe. **On the other hand, people say they don't believe in God because they cannot see God.** "Thou believest that there is one; thou doest well: the devils also believe, and tremble." **My friend, God does exits!** (James 2:19)

Can I ask you something: do you know Satan exits? How do you know that? My friend, it is on my mind to say this again, people say that they do not believe in God, but no man can ever create a living thing into existence. **Man was created just like how nature was created for man; therefore man cannot be the creator. The story of evolution is totally false. Nothing in this entire universe is by chance.** Look at the perfect ecosystem and food chain, and the structure of the universe. **All these things work hand in hand. There must be a higher power Yes, the Heavenly Father. Scientists say the universe was created by gases such as nitrogen and oxygen that explains living things such as animals, plants and even humans.**

But they fail to answer who creates the gases and the perfect balance of nature. **So they know the truth but as I said, they are out to deceive you.** The opening statement of the Bible declares that **"In the beginning God created the heavens and the earth."** (Genesis 1:1-31) Contemporary science although not absolutely certain on exactly when, has theorized that the universe did in fact have a beginning with what is known as **"The Big Bang."** **It flies in the face of common sense for anyone to assert that absolute nothing could produce something. That is foolishness. Without a beginning, nothing can be produced!** Thus it is more reasonable to infer that God is that something with no beginning which produced everything that we know of which has a beginning.

The Bible says, "He stretches out the north over empty place, and hangeth the earth upon nothing." (Job 26:7-14) Perhaps only divine revelation could account for the Bible's accuracy in detailing these and other facts about our universe far in advance of us developing the technology to verify such assertions. **My friend, God exists. Believe it, know it: He is truly real.** Is it true that we cannot see God? Yes, the Bible says no woman or man or child, can see God. For this reason the Bible condemns images of God. (John 1:18; Exodus 20:4-5; 33:20) Let me give you an example. You say that God does not exist, because you cannot see him.

Think about this. **Can you see the wind? No! Nobody can see the wind, but you can see the things the wind does. You can see the leaves moving when the wind blows through the branches of a tree. So you believe that there is wind?** Yes, you can see the things God has done too. When you see a living flower or a bird, you see something that God has made. Men can make a house. But no man can make Human Nature. True! **So then believe God exist, just as you believe wind exist and you cannot see it.**

It can be proven that God existed "today" **If Jesus had died, and stayed dead, we would have had to say, "God doesn't exist." But Jesus came back to life and lives today.**

This is the biggest claim for the existence of God, and it is understandably also the most controversial claim debated among people today. The message Jesus communicated with us is the same today as it always has been. **Jesus, came so that people might have life, and have it to the fullest.** My friend you must believe that God is real because no one can please God without faith, for whoever comes to God must have faith that God exists and rewards those who seek him. (Hebrews. 11: 6) **So have faith now!**

So, my friend, do you believe that there really is a God. Someone might ask you, who made the Sun and the Earth? Show them in your Bible at Genesis 1:1 that says: God created the Heaven and the Earth. **Yes God made all these wonderful things! How do you feel about that? Isn't it wonderful to be alive? We can see the beautiful flowers and the other things that God has made.** And we can eat the foods that God has given us. For all those things, we should thank God. Most of all, we should thank him for giving us life. If you are really thankful to God, will you do what He says to do in the Bible? In that way you show that you love the One who made all things. **"God is a Spirit: and they that worship him must worship him in spirit and in truth."** (John 4:24; 13:14; 14:23)

The Bible tells us that God said: Now we will make human beings: They will be like us and resemble us. (Genesis 1:26) Do you know whom God was talking to? He was taking to his Son Jesus. **Perhaps someone may ask you if you believe in God** what will you say to them? **Why not point to a house, then ask the person who made the house?** The house certainly did not make itself! The Bible said: "Every house is builded by some man; but he that built all things is God." (Hebrews 3:4) You should show appreciation to God for all He has done. And stop saying God does not exist. **Stop being ungrateful.** To know if God exist, you have to experience God for yourself. However, for those who believe without experiences, praise the LORD God.

To learn more get the book called **"Enlightening You: The Lies Told by Some Pastors"** My advice **to those people who do not believe in God; who say that God doesn't exist:** God said that the fearful, and unbelieving, and the abominable have their part in the lake of fire. **So if you don't want this to happen to you ask God to ravel himself to you, and you will know that God is real, and he can save you from this place.** (Revelation 21:8) Read some more Bible text that give strong; conviction. Read (Romans 12:17-21; 1 Peter 3:10-14)

"Ah LORD GOD! Behold, thou hast made the heaven and the earth by thy great power and stretched out arm, and there is nothing too hard for thee." (Jeremiah 32:17)

CHAPTER 9

It is Not Right to Get Even, Why?

Most people like to act big and dangerous. Do you like to be with such people? **Won't you prefer be with people who want to be kind and want peace?** Do you know what Jesus said about this? **"Blessed are the peace makers: for they shall be called the children of God."** (Matthew 5:9) But sometimes, other people do things to aggravate us by getting us angry. Isn't that true? **So we may feel like getting even with them, don't you?**

My friend, this happened once to Jesus' disciples when they were traveling towards Jerusalem. Let me tell you about it. When they had gone some distance, Jesus sent a few of his

FROM WORLDLY TO CHRISTIAN WISDOM AND TRUTH

disciples ahead of him, who went into a village in Samaria to get everything ready for them to rest. **But the people there would not receive him, because the Samaritans had a different religion. And they didn't like anyone that went to the city of Jerusalem to worship.** If that had happened to you, what would you have done to them? Would you not get angry, and want to get even with them? That is what the disciples, James and John wanted to do. They said to Jesus: **"Lord, wilt thou that we command fire to come down from heaven, and consume them, even as Elias did?"**

No, wonder Jesus called them "the Sons of Thunder." But Jesus turned and rebuked them, and said, **"Ye know not what manner of spirit ye are of. For the Son of man is not come to destroy men's lives, but to save them."** In other words: **Jesus is saying: it was not right to treat other people bad if they treat you bad.** (Luke 9:51-56; Mark 3:17) My friends, to learn more about how to love your enemies unconditionally, get the book, **"The Only True Way to Demonstrate Love and Its Meaning"** My friend, it is true that people may be mean to us at times. Other people may not want us to be around them, they will not want to talk to us. **They may even say: We hate you and we wish you were dead!** When something like that happens to you, it can make you feel bad and emotional. **You may feel like doing something to get even with them.** But should you? The Bible can help us at Proverbs 24:29: "Say not, I will do so to him as he hath done to me: I will render to the man according to his work." What does that mean to you? **It is saying that it is wrong to get even, or take revenge.**

Can you remember what the Bible said about this: **"Blessed are the peace makers: for they shall be called the children of God."** (Matthew 5:9) Do you remember the Scriptures also says, **"Therefore if thine enemy hunger, feed him; if he thirst, give him drink: for in so doing, thou shalt heap coals of fire on his head.** Be not overcome of evil, but overcome evil with good." **My friend, by doing good for your enemies they will burn with shame. It also encourages you to "Love your enemies, bless them that curse you, do good to them that hate you, and pray for them which despitefully use you, and persecute you."** (Romans 12:20-21; Matthew 5:44) Jesus showed, those who are the true 'Sons of God' imitate God's love even towards their enemies.

My friend, you should not be mean to a person just because he was mean to you. **But what if someone tries to pick a fight with you? He may try to get you angry by calling you names.** He may laugh at you and say that you are scared. Suppose he calls you a coward. **What should you do? Should you let yourself get into a ridiculous fight?** Let's see what the Bible has to say about this: get your Bible turned to Matthew 5:39 read what Jesus says: It's not me, but Jesus who says: **"That ye resist not evil: but whosoever shall smite thee on thy right cheek, turn to him the other also."**

My friend, what do you think Jesus meant by that? Did he mean that if someone hits you with his fist on one side of your face, you should tell him hit you on the other side? No! What he simply means, **if one person tried to make a confrontation with a literal slap, or with hurtful words, you should avoid retaliating. Instead, you should attempt to avoid what could become a vicious circle of rendering evil for evil.** (Romans 12:17) Truly Jesus didn't mean that if his followers are struck on one side of the face, they should stagger to their feet and offer the other side as a target. **My friend: "Say not, I will do so to him, as he hath done to me: I will render to the man according to his work."** (Proverbs 24:29)

[That is humility, my friend] A person may slap you to pick a fight. He wants you to get angry. And if you get angry and you push or shove back, what will happen? You will probably get into a fight. My friend, Jesus did not want his disciples to get into fights. **So he said that if someone slaps you, you should not slap him back.** You should not become angry and get into a fight. **If you do, you show that you are no better than the one who started the fight.** If trouble such as fights, disagreements, or conflict should start, what do you think is the right thing to do? **The right thing to do is walk or run away.** The other person may push or shove you a few more times. But that will probably be the end of it. When you walk or run away, it does not mean that you are weak.

It means that you are strong for what God has said is right. God says: **"Blessed is the man who endures temptation, for when he is tried, he shall receive the crown of life, which the Lord hath promised to them that love him."** (James 1:12; Luke 10:19) But what if you let yourself get into a fight and you win? What could happen then? The one you beat up could come back with some friends. They might even hurt you and you might have to go to the hospital. **So, can you see now why Jesus did not want us to get into fights?** What should you do if you do see other people fighting? Should you take side with one or the other?

My friend, getting involved in an argument that is none of your business is like going down the street and grabbing a dog by the ears. It would hurt the dog, and he would snap at you, wouldn't he? The more the dog tries to get loose, the harder you would have to hold on to the ears and the more excited the dog would become. If you let him go, he would probably bite you hard. **But can you just stand there and hold his ears forever?** Well, that is the kind of trouble that you would be in if you get mixed up in fights between other people. You may not know who started the fight or why they are fighting.

The best thing to do is go to the Bible at (Proverbs 27:12) that said: **"A prudent man foreseeth the evil, and hideth himself; but the simple pass on, and are punished."** Be peaceful my friend. True disciples of Jesus do all they can to avoid getting into fights. In this way you show that you are strong for what is right. The Bible says that **"And the servant of the Lord must not strive; but be gentle unto all men, apt to teach, patient."** (2 Timothy 2:24)

One Love!

CHAPTER 10

Do You Always Want to Be First?
Humility and Hospitality, get it!

This is an age in which people lack humility and hospitality and love to be first in everything. **They don't mind pushing someone away so that they can be first in line. Even in our churches, people behave like this.** Have you seen this happen? Jesus Christ saw grown-ups trying to get the prominent or most important places. He **did not like that at all.** Let's see what happened. Jesus was invited to a big meal at the home of a Pharisee, who was an important religious leader. **After he arrived, he noticed how some of the guests chose to take the best places, and manifested no kind of hospitality,** so he told a story to all of them who had been invited.

Jesus said: **When someone invites you to a wedding feast, do not sit-down in the best place.** It could happen that someone more important than you may have been invited, and your host, who will have to come and say to you, 'Let him have this place.' **Then you could be embarrassed by having to sit in the lowest place.** Therefore, when you are invited, choose to sit in the lowest place, so that your host may come to you and say, 'Come on up, my friend, to a better place.' **Isn't that Humility and Hospitality?** This will bring you honor in the presence of all the other guests. Jesus said: **"For whosoever exalteth himself shall be abased; and he that humbleth himself shall be exalted."** (Luke 14:11)

My friend, did you get the point of Jesus' story? Let me give you an example to see if you did. Imagine that you are getting on a crowded bus. Should you rush to get in a seat and let an older woman stand? **Would Jesus like this? No!** Someone may say that it does not make any difference to Jesus what we do. But do you believe that? When Jesus was at the big meal at the home of the Pharisee, **he noticed the people as they chose their seats.** Jesus is just as interested in what we do today. Now that Jesus is in heaven, he certainly is in a good position to notice us. **When someone tries to be first, it can cause trouble. Often there is an argument and people get angry.** Sometimes this happens when children go for a bus ride together.

As soon as the bus doors are opened, the children rush in to be first. They want the best seats; the ones near the window. What may happen then? Well, they may get mad at one another. **Wanting to be first can cause lots of problems.** It even caused trouble among Jesus' apostles. They argued among themselves about who was the greatest. (Mark 9:33-34; John 13:2-14) What did Jesus do then? He corrected them. But later they had another argument. Let's see how it started. The apostles, along with others, were traveling with Jesus for the last time to the city of Jerusalem. **Jesus had been talking to them about his kingdom. James and John had seriously been thinking about ruling as Kings with Jesus.** They had even spoken to their mother, Salome, about it. (Matthew 27:56; Mark 15:40)

So when they were on their way to Jerusalem, Salome came to Jesus with her two sons, bowed before him, and asked him for a favor. "What wilt thou?" Jesus asked her. She answered, **"Grant that these my two sons may sit, the one on thy right hand, and the other on the life, in thy kingdom."** Well, when the other ten apostles learnt about James and John's mother's request, it made them very upset. Jesus then gave all of his apostles some good advice. He called them all together and said, "You know that the rulers of the heathen have power over them, and the leaders have complete authority. This is not the way it shall be among you."

Jesus continued: **And if one of you wants to be first, he must be a slave-like the Son of Man who did not come to** be served, but to serve and to give his life to redeem many people. Think about that! (Matthew 20:20-28) Do you know what a slave does? He serves other people, not expecting others to serve him. He takes the lowest place, not the first place. **He acts as the least important one, not the most important one.** And remember, Jesus said that the one who wants to be first should act like a slave toward others.

Now, what do you think that means for you? **Would a slave argue with his master over who is going to get the best seat? Or, would he argue about who is going to eat first? What do you think?** Jesus explained that a slave always puts his master before himself. (Luke 17:7-10) So, my friend, rather than trying to be first, you should be like a slave toward others. That means putting others ahead of yourself. **It also means considering others as being more important than yourself.** Can you think of ways that you can put others first? Look for some of the ways that you can put others first by serving them. Help elderly people, and those in need.

Also, help your family. You will remember that Jesus Christ put others ahead of himself by serving them. **The last evening he spent with his apostles, he even got down and washed their feet.** If you put others first by serving them, you will be pleasing Christ Jesus and his Heavenly Father, the Most High God. **WHAT IS TRUE HUMILITY?** Read these Bible texts for your answers: Zephaniah 3:12; Matthew 18:4; Titus 3:2; Psalm 51:3-4.

HOW DID GOD'S SONMANIFEST HUMILITY?
(Zechariah9:9; Philippians 2;5-11; Hebrews 2:9; Matthew 11:29; Psalm 18:27; Psalm 138: 6; Psalm 147:6; Isaiah 29:19)

A PROMISE FROM GOD: Those who exalt themselves will be humbled, and those who humble themselves will be exalted. (Matthew 23:12)

HOW SHOULD I SHOW OTHERS HOSPITALITY?
See these Bible texts for your answers: (Genesis19:2; Genesis 24:32; 1 peter 4: 9)

TO WHOM SHOULD I BE HOSPITABLE? (Romans 12:13; Hebrews 13:2; Isaiah 58:7; Luke 14;12-14; Hebrews 13:2)

My encouragement to you is to always put others ahead of yourself. Help one another, love one another. Be loving, kind, peaceful, to everyone. Read (Luke 9:48; Romans 12:3 and Philippians 2:3-5) For more encouragement, **email** me at **truthofsalvation463@ymail.com** or add me to **Skype**, my Skype name: **Jesusiscomingyou**

CHAPTER 11

Does God Approve Of Those
Parties Today?

Do you like to go parties? They can be lots of excitement and fun. Do you think Jesus would want you (us) to go to parties? Yes he will. **Well, he wants you to attend good parties, like when someone is getting married.** Jesus and some of his disciples went to a party. God is happy when you enjoy yourself at a good party. (John 2:1-11)

The Bible tells us that God parted the Red Sea to let the Israelites pass through. Do you remember reading that in the Bible? Afterward, the people **sang and danced and gave thanks to God. It was like a party.** The people there were very happy, and you can be sure that God was very happy as well.

And He approved of this party. (Exodus 15:1-21) A couple of years later, the Israelites went to another party. **This time the people who invited them did not even worship God.** They even bowed themselves down to worship other gods and went on to have sexual relations with people to whom they were not married. **Today people behave like this! Do you think it was all right to attend a party like that?**

God did not approve of this party. The Israelites ate the food and worshipped the god, called Baal. **God was very angry with them, and said Moses, "Take all them who disobey me and execute them in broad daylight and I will no longer be angry."** (Numbers 25:1-9; 1 Corinthians 10:8) What does this tell you? **It simply means that God, the Father only approved of party that glorified and respected Him. There must be righteousness in the party.** Today's parties have killing, sex and immoral things such as drugs and music that glorify the Devil. These are the kinds of parties that anger God. The Bible said: **"He that believeth on the Son hath everlasting life; and he that believeth not the Son shall not see life; but the wrath of God abideth on Him.** (John 3:36)

It means if you obey God's will, you will not be executed, but if you disobey Him and attend these immoral parties, you will fall into condemnation. Do you remember the two birthday parties the Scriptures talk about? Both of these birthday parties were for men who did not serve God. **Do you remember the birthday party of king Herod Antipas?** Yes! He was the ruler of the district of Galilee where Jesus once lived. **King Herod did many evil things. He took the wife of his brother and married her.** Her name was Herodias, and he did many other wrong things. God's servant John reprimanded the Governor and said to him, **"It is not lawful for thee to have thy brother's wife." Herod ordered John's arrest and shut him up in prison.** (Luke 3:19-20)

While John was in prison, the day came for the celebration of Herod's birth. Herod gave a big party. He invited top government officials, the military chiefs and the leading citizens of Galilee. They all ate and drank and enjoyed themselves. Then the daughter of Herodias came in and danced, and pleased Herod and his guests. The King in appreciation said to the girl, "What would you like to have?" He said to her: **"I sware unto you, whatsoever thou shalt ask of me, I will give to thee, unto the half of my kingdom."** The girl did not know what to ask for, so she went and asked her mother, "What shall I ask?"

Now Herodias hated John the Baptist very much s**o she told her daughter to ask for the head of John the Baptist. The girl came straightway with unto the king, and asked:** "I will that thou give me by and by in a charger the head of John the Baptist" **King Herod was exceedingly sorry, for he did not want to kill John because he knew that John was a good holy man.** But Herod had made an oath (promise). He could not refuse her because of the vows he had made in front of all his guests. **And immediately the king sent his** executioner, with orders for John's head to be brought in a charger and gave it to the girl, who gave it to her mother. **Do you think God was happy with this, or approved of this party?** No!(Mark 6:17-29)

The other birthday party that the Bible tells us about wasn't any better. It was for a king of Egypt. During this party the king had someone's head chopped off. Then, after that, he hanged the man's body on a pole, for the birds to eat his flesh. (Genesis 40:19-22) **Do you think that God approved of those two parties?** My friend, **would you have wanted to be present at one of them?** You know that everything in the Bible is there for a reason. It tells us about just two birthday parties. And at both parties bad, evil things were part of the celebration. **So, what would you say that God is telling us about parties? He wants parties which glorify His name and not the Devil. He does not want us to sin at parties or worship another gods but him.**

The name was given to Moses, is "I Am," the only true living God. God is love and He does not want us to entertain ourselves in such immoral parties. **It is true that at parties today, people do not cut off someone's head, but they argue and hurt one another, do drugs and alcohol, and have sex with unmarried partners, or even strangers.** To sum it all up, we need to worship the true God, the Heavenly Father, the Most High God. **In today's parties, people practice homosexually, immorality, violence, and play songs that worship Satan.**

My friend, stay away from such parties; they will only bring destruction to your soul. So when you have parties, make sure that they are good ones in God's eyes. The Bible says: '**It is better to go to a home where there is mourning than to one where there is a party, because the living should always remind, themselves that death is waiting for us all.**" Also, "Sorrow is better than laughter, it may sadden your face, but it sharpens your understanding. **Someone who is always thinking about happiness is a fool. A wise person thinks about death.**" (Ecclesiastes 7:2-4)

The importance of always doing what God approves is also shown at Proverbs 12:2; John 8:29-32; Romans 12:2; and 1 John 3:21; also John 14:15 and Ecclesiastes 7:5-7

One Love!

CHAPTER 12

Christian, Will All Good People Be Saved?

All over the world we have heard people say, "God will save all good people." This **implies** that good people in all **churches, temples, mosques, etc** will be saved. It also implies that there may be good people who have never been members of any church who will also be saved. Will all good people be saved? What does the Bible say? **The Bible teaches that: "For by grace are ye saved through faith; and that not of yourselves: it is the gift of God: not of works, lest any man should boast."** If people could be saved by their good deeds, then it would not have been necessary for Jesus Christ to die for our sins. (Ephesians 2:8-10)

My friend, Apostle Paul also wrote: "For when we were ye without strength, in due time Christ died for the ungodly. For scarcely a righteous man will die; perhaps for a good man someone would even dare to die. But God commended his love toward us, in that while we were yet sinners Christ died for us." In other words: **We were helpless and hopeless, but Jesus died for the wicked at the time that God chose.** Jesus didn't die for the righteous one, but for the unrighteous. **It is a difficult thing for someone to die for an unrighteous person. It may even be that someone might dare to die for a good person.** But God has shown us how much he loves us unconditionally-it was while we were still sinners that Christ died for us! (Romans 5:6-8)

The Scripture teaches that to be saved, we must confess with our mouth Jesus is Lord and believe in our heart that God has raised Him from the dead, we will then be saved. **For it is by our faith that we are put right with God; it is by our confession that we are saved.** Not by goodness. **"Whoever believes in him will not be disappointed."** Read and understand, my friend! (Romans 10:9-11) Even the very best people, who have lived long enough to know the difference between right and wrong, have sinned. The Bible says: **"What then? Are we better than they? No, in no wise: for we have before proved both Jews Gentiles that they are all under sin."** As the Scriptures says: "There is none righteous, no, not one." Everyone has sinned and is far away from God's saving presence. (Romans 3:9-10, 23)

My friend, in chapter 10 of the Book of Acts, we read about a man named Cornelius. Cornelius was a very good man. He was also a very religious man. **He and his whole family worshiped God. He also did much to help the Jewish poor people and was constantly praying to God.** But he was not saved. Please notice the Bible's description of this good man. (Acts 10:1-2) In spite of his faith and good deeds, Cornelius was not saved. He was told by an angel of God to send someone to Joppa for a man whose full name is Simon Peter. **He will speak words to you by which you and all your family will be saved.** (Acts 11:13-14) Will all good people be saved? The answer is "No!" for even the best people has sinned and **just one sin can keep a person out of heaven.**

John wrote, but nothing that is impure will enter the City, or anyone who does shameful things or tells lies. **Only those whose names are written in the Lamb's book of (life) living will enter the City.** (Revelation 21:27) **This is done in your obedience to the Gospel of Christ Jesus.** Please read (Acts 22: 16) and now, why wait any longer? Get up and be baptized and have your sins washed away by calling on the name of Jesus Christ. Not all good people will be saved. Neither will all religious people be saved. **It is not enough to be good or religious, but one must be saved by the blood of Jesus.**

For example: Jesus said: when the Day of Judgment comes; many will say to me, 'Lord, Lord! In your name we spoke God's message, by your name we drove out many demons and performed many miracles!' **Then I will profess unto them, I never knew you: Depart (or get from me), ye that work iniquity, or wicked people!** My friend, do you know why? Because they do not teach God's will, they teach man-made rules. (Matthew 7:21-23) Jesus said: "Every plant which my Father in heaven did not plant will be pulled up," (Matthew 15:13) He also said: **"Not everyone who calls me 'Lord, Lord' will enter the kingdom of Heaven, but only those who do what my Father in heaven wants them to do."**

My friend, some people will be saved. **Those who will be saved are those who humbly submit to our Lord Jesus Christ in Obedience to his Gospel and who live for him and do his will.** But even though Jesus was God's Son, he learned through his sufferings to be obedient. **And having been perfected, Jesus became the source of eternal salvation for all those who obey him.** (Hebrews 5: 8-9) Dear reader, have you obeyed the gospel of Jesus Christ? If you have not, you are lost! **Please don't say I love people and I do well, it is very good to do such things, but if you don't give Jesus your heart, all will be in vain.**

Please obey Christ today. Arise, and be baptized, and wash away your sins, calling on the living name of Christ Jesus. **Believe that Jesus is the only savior. Behold in the Lamb of God, who takes away the sins of the world.** Christ said: "I am the way, the truth, and the life, no man cometh unto the Father, but by me." (John 14:6)

Prayer

My friend say, this prayer after me, Heavenly Father, I know that I have sinned and need your forgiveness. **I believe that your Son the Lord Jesus Christ died for me on the cross and I am willing to repent and turn from my sins.** Father I welcome the Holy Spirit into my life to take full control and I vow to live my life to please you from this day on. **I confess with my mouth, Jesus is Lord," and believe in my heart that God raised him from the dead,** 'I now by faith invite the Lord Jesus Christ to come into my heart and life as my personal savior and I am willing, by your grace, to follow and obey him as the Lord of my life. Amen. **My friend, you have now received salvation!** As the Scripture says, **"Whosoever believeth on him shall not be ashamed."** (Roman 10: 9-11)

Signed.. Date...........................

Congratulations to you, you have been saved. If you sincerely say this prayer, from your soul. God will save you; He will save you, Blessed!

CHAPTER 13

The Power and Influence of Music Lucifer Was In Charge Of the Music in Heaven

W hen we were in the world [unsaved], my friend, Music was one of our masters. You can read in the Bible where it says: "No man can serve two masters: for either he will hate the one, and love the other; or else he will hold to the one, and despise the other. Ye cannot serve God and mammon." **My friend, you cannot serve both God and Satan.** (Matthew 6:24) **Music has the power to control your emotions, it may comfort you, or give you false hope, freeing your mind temporally, make you feel sad or hurt or even violent and angry.** Music is **POWERFUL.**

Because music is so powerful we need to educate ourselves on the history, the spirit and the purpose behind music. **Music was first used in heaven as an tool of praise and worship towards God the Father.** God created Lucifer and all the other angels in heaven, Lucifer was the angel of music. God entrusted total power in Lucifer. When Lucifer played music, the angels in heaven worshipped God. **The truth is, music is really to glorify God and his greatness. But Lucifer became Satan because he got jealous of God and greedy for power.** He wanted to overthrow God; he influenced some angels in heaven to worship him as the supreme.

God Almighty, Powerful Father of all things, could not allow this to happen, so he cast Satan along with all those who were influenced by Satan, out of heaven. As a result, Satan is now roaming the earth to find souls to deceive and to influence people into worshiping him, just like the angels in heaven. He does everything for us to stop worshiping God, the loving Creator: **He even uses today's singers. He lies to you in the music to entrap your mind and heart. Music is a potent weapon as it is in the 'Universal Language.'** For example: You can hear a song in Spanish and like it, even though you don't know how to speak or understand Spanish. If you like it, you could start singing it and **blindly worship the Devil. "Guard your heart and mind diligently" from** the Devil and what you allow in your mind from the media such as TV, Internet and Radio. **Everything you allow into your mind influence your view of life.**

All The Statement Is Alleged! It Is Facts!

Today, Satan is killing millions more through the influence of music, such as **Rock and Roll, Hip-Hop, Rap, Pop, Soca and Dancehall. These popular types of music, along with many more, are used to glorify sex and drugs by the Devil.** This cause people to act irresponsibly, encouraging diseases that destroy many lives. You will see the true picture beyond such music. **The lyrics may encourage sexual promiscuity and give you comfort, but it is the wrong kind of comfort. You need comfort from the Lord Jesus Christ.** Just like in heaven, what makes you think the angel of music, Satan is not using what God has blessed him with as a weapon, drawing worship against God. **It is the only well-known weapon he has and is the only one he needs.**

Rock and Roll singer, Gene Simmons:

Let's all face the fact worldly music gave us advice on what to do. **When you so-call "love" these singers and make them your idol you are calling them your false god.** Hence if you love these people so much you would indirectly do what they do; speak like them, and dress like them. They become your role-model w**hen, in fact, Jesus should be that role model in your active life.** Have you ever heard about the Rock and Roller, Gene Simmons?: He sings, **"I have always wondered what human flesh tastes like, and I've always wanted to be a cannibal."**

He wants to be God, not only a cannibal. God has banned us from drinking blood or eating human flesh, yet still he says this. **Now tell me, can you follow two masters?** You can only really love one! **The lust to be God is the trait of his master, the Devil.** He said, "If God is such hot stuff, then why is he afraid to have other gods before him?" . . . "I always wanted to be God." **(Circus, Sept, 13, 1976, pg. 42). Can you see Satan is using him to blaspheme God. So should we listen to his music?** Another person, hip hop artist, Jay-z, along with Gene Simmons, echo Aleister Crowley's satanic doctrine. **"Do what thou wilt"** He says: "People are going to tell you, "You can't do this. You can't do that. They can all go [Expletive] themselves . . . you don't need them—around, and that includes your parents . . . Get rid of those leeches . . ."

You see he is teaching you and your child to be disobedient to God, and have no kind of respect at all for anyone, but God's words say: "Children, it is your duty to obey your parents in the Lord. Respect your father and mother." (Ephesians 6:1-4) You can see he is against God, and Satan is using him to mislead you and your children. **Take a note of singers you love and admire. You see and hear them but are their lives really in accordance with God's ordinances?** No is the answer! For example

Peter Chris's said:

"I find myself evil. I believe in the Devil as much as God." He said: "You can use either one to get things done." (Faces, Dec-1984). That is deception, my friend. In Matthew 4:8, this is what happened: **Then Satan took Jesus to a very high mountain and showed him all the kingdom of the world in all their greatness.** Satan said **"I will give you this, if you kneel down and worship me."** In the same way today the Devil comes to people and says the same thing. But God commanded us in Exodus 20: 1-3: **"I am the LORD thy God, which have brought thee out of the land of Egypt, out of the house of bondage. Thou shalt have no other gods before me."**

These so-called stars worship Satan and birth his will into the minds of the hearers in return for wealth, power, fame and beauty (etc). **If you want wealth and fame, you can get it from Jesus Christ, but my friend, this is not important; eternal life is. If you worship Satan you may get wealth and fame as well, but you will not get eternal life; you will instead end up in eternal fire and damnation.** (Luke 4: 5-8) My friend, if Satan wants people to worship him, what do you think he will do for them? Satan said **"All this power will I give thee, and the glory of them: for that is delivered unto me; and to whomsoever I will I give it. If thou therefore wilt worship me, all shall be thine."** (Luke 4: 5-8)

This is deception my friend. Hence the kind of influence these very talented and famous people have on the behavior of the children in the world, manifesting violence and lack of self-control. **Their magical tunes and lyrics secretly entice your soul and body into worshiping Satan. They are not to be trusted as their influence on writing songs, singing and making crazy and seductive music videos all come from a very high Satanic supernatural power.** Another artist you may know about is Prince. This is not just for the few artists we discuss now or a certain genre of music. The Devil may use any cultural music to do so. Once the music contains evil lyrics and promotes sex, lies and drugs, it is wrong!

Pop artist Prince sang in 1999: Kiss is a Rock and Roll, singer

The pop artist, Prince with sales of over two hundred million albums, has influenced all kind of people, and, under the influence of Satanic Spirit-beings, has misled many people worldwide. Prince says **"I have a spirit living inside me and we have not determined what kind of spirit is that."** Prince even changed his name because the Spirit enters his body and he feels the spirit will not like him being called, Prince, so he finally flips this name backwards. Prince even practices homosexuality and calls his band, "the revolution."

Prince's Song, "1999" appears to be about refusing to repent in the end time. It states: "I was dreaming when I wrote this so forgive me if it goes astray" **What! What!** "But when I wake up in the morning" "I could have sworn it was judgment day" **Prince goes on to sing about the coming destruction and he did not really care,** and he is Going and party through 1999, 2000. He sings: "The sky was all purple. There were people running everywhere. Trying to run from the destruction. But you know I didn't even care. 2000 zero, party over, oops, out of time. So tonight I'm Gonne' Party like its 1999." **Prince says he is going to party until judgment day.** But do you know what 1999means? Antichrist's number. **You may wonder how I know that! You will see how I know.**

My friend, look at that the cover of Prince's album, '1999'. In the middle of it we see 'Prince' in the revelation written backwards. We also see the [P] for prince, turned upside down as a flame. When the album is inverted, we see more to the picture: the number 666 which is the number of the antichrist and with a Valid pointed down and 'prince' backwards makes it **EVIL.** The upside down [P] denotes fire and destruction. **The demons are using Prince and other Rock and Rollers and Pop-stars who are seeking to bring the world under the antichrist's control,** and then to destruction in Hell. Prince changed his name for a period of time b**ecause he said the other being living in him might not like the name, 'Prince', so he called himself, Evil.** You can see this in the picture below.

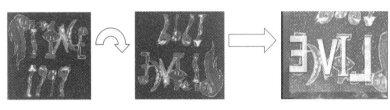

Notice Upside Down it's 666 with a down arrow (EVIL) and a Flame

My friend, Protect Yourself against Satan, his demons and his influences through music. **How can you protect yourself against wicked musical influences?** The Bible answers: **"Submit yourselves therefore to God. Resist the devil, and he will flee from you."** (James 4:7) Put on all the armor that God gives you, so that you will be able to stand up against Satan evil tricks (Ephesians 6:11). In other words, we heed that injunction when we live by the teaching found in the Bible, the only sacred book that fully exposes Satan, and his demons, and their crafty acts.

My friend, in order to keep Satan from getting the upper hand over you: for we are not ignorant of his devices. (2 Corinthians 2:11) The Bible also tells us that the influence Satan, have on us God will soon crush Satan under our feet's forever. (Romans 16:20) **"For the upright shall dwell in the land, and the perfect shall remain in it."** (Proverbs 2:21) Can you understand the Bible is warning you not to imitate these singers? **The Scripture is giving you advice power and wisdom to over-come Satan and his influences, take it!** **Here's a**nother person you may know called Kiss.

Kiss is a Rock and Roll, Singer Too:

Kiss sings about being the incubus [a sex demon] who implants the egg. Their video then cuts into a young girl. "I am the incubus I lay the egg in you, the worm that burrows through your brain." [Kiss is Mortal] **God did not spare the angels who sinned, but threw them into hell, where they are kept chained in darkness, waiting for the Day of Judgment. The devil** is using his demons, to influence people on earth, so you can imagine what he'll do if he goes free. **That is why they are so many young women who are sinning against their bodies.** In the beginning when God created mankind and they had spread all over the world, and girls were being born, some of the heavenly beings saw that these girls were beautiful, so they took the ones they liked. **They were no longer called angels, but Sex demons, so you can imagine, why Kiss calls himself the Sex demon, and the one who implants the egg.** (James 2:4; Genesis 6:1-4)

My friend, Kiss sings about being the Lord of the flies [a name for Satan], the left Hand Path [a term used for Satanism] and the father of lies [a description]**So you can see he is confessing that he is a worshipper of Satan, and is misleading people, through the Power of music.** The Bible says: "Professing themselves to be wise, they became fools, And changed the glory of the uncorruptible God into an image made like to corruptible man, and to birds, and fourfooted beasts, and creeping things." (Romans 1:22-24) Jesus said in

John 8:44: **"Ye are of your father the devil, and the lusts of your father ye will do.** He was a murderer from the beginning, and abode not in the truth, because there is no truth in him. When he speaketh a lie, he speaketh of him own: foe he is a liar, and the father of it."

When someone lies, will you trust them? When Kiss says he is the lord of the flies, he is saying Satan is in him. So he is not to be trusted. Kiss sings: "I'm the Lord of the Flies you know I'm unholy, from the left hand of power comes the father of lies." Do you know who the father of lies is? **Yes Satan the Devil, Kiss is unholy, just like his father Satan, so you can see where they get the power from.** Kiss pays homage to Satan as the god of Rock and Roll in his song, he sings god of Thunder. **He confesses that Satan is the god of Rock and Roll, so should we listen to these Rock and Roll singers?**

If Satan is their leader, and we listen to these Rock and roll singers, he will become our leader too. **If Satan is a deceiver, why listen to his singers, these singers will deceive you into worshipping Satan.** Kiss said: "I was raised by the demons trained to rein as the god of thunder and Rock and Roll. **The spell you're under will slowly rob you of your virgin soul"** **Please don't allow him to do that to you!** Open your eyes! Another influential artist was Michael Jackson.

Michael Jackson the king of Pop

One of the most influential artist of all times was Michael Jackson, the king of Pop. Michael Jackson who it is said has sold over seven hundred million albums and influenced multitudes all over the world: **Michael Jackson gathered hundreds of millions of fans, and he eventually become increasingly sinister. After Michael Jackson had much of the world firmly in his grasp, he began promoting violence through his video and music.** Michael Jackson helped to open the door to the violence that became the back bone to Rap music. **Michael Jackson also opened up himself to the occult, as seen in 'Thriller' and denied his evolvement, but later admissions contradicted his denial.**

These artistes are influenced by Satanic Spirit-beings, which influence Satan words. Michael used people as puppets, just like many other artistes. There is very good evidence that Michael was influenced by Satan. **Michael Jackson sang, "We are the world, we are the children."** MY FRIEND, all these different artistes joined together, singing, "We are the world, we are the children". **These words were actually given by Satan, totally contradict the word of God, and fitted into what the Bible says Satan will be doing in the End-time.** Let us read about this, from the Bible:

Jesus says **"If the world hates you, just remember that it has hates me first. If** you belonged to the world, then the world would love you as its own." **Michael sang, "We are the world."** My Christian brother and sister, we are not of the world, remember the world hates us. Remember what the apostle John said to us: **"And we know that we are of God, and the whole world lieth in wickedness."** (1John 5:19) **My friend, if the world is under the power of Satan, and we are the world then, Satan has power to influence us too.** Michael knew that but, he sang, **"We are the world."** He was working for Satan. **Jesus said that he was not of the world, but that it hated him, because he kept telling it that its ways were bad.** What did Jesus mean?

Let's see, Jesus said: **"My kingdom is not of the world: if my kingdom were of this world, then would my servants fight, that I should not be delivered to the Jews:** but now is my kingdom not from hence." (John 18:36-38) You will learn more about the song called we are the world, **so you will know and learn the truth beyond music.** Read John 15:18-22; John 8:44, and John 7:6-7. Aleister Crowley (1875-1947), one of the most evil men that ever lived, practised magic, and did immoral things. (Revelation 21: 8) **Satanist Aleister Crowley had a special secret room filled with mirrors where he practiced black magic and contacted spirit beings.**

Like Alester Crowley, Michael Jackson also used a secret room of mirrors to conjure spirits. **Michael Jackson admitted that in this room he contacted Leebarche. Michael Jackson revealed** "I have my own secret room, with a moving wall and mirrors. That's where I talk to **Leebarche**; this is the Voice I hear in there. **I feel his presence so very close to me." He added: He is like my guardian angel. He gives me permission to record his theme Song "I'll be seeing you."** (News Feb 14 1987). Yes he will be seeing him, in the lake of fire! **Satan is using them to lead the souls of men and women into destruction, so how could we listen to Michael Jackson, who conjured spirits, and even prayed to them.**

That is not right! His intentions were to mislead or damage you. God said: "When thou prayest, enter into thy closet, and when thou hast shut thy door, pray to the Father which seeth in secret shall reward thee openly." (Matthew 6:6) **Michael Jackson got his songs from the spirit world. He** said "I wake up from dreams and go wow! Put this down on paper! The whole thing is strange. You hear the words; everything is right there in front of your face. And you say to yourself I'm sorry I just didn't write this. It's there already. It is all been done, somewhere, someplace. **I'm the courier bringing it into the world."** (Newsweek, Jan 10, 1983, pg.53)

My friend, it appears that the demonic beings energized Michael Jackson when he hit the stage. Michael Jackson said: **"When I hit the stage it's all of a sudden a magic from somewhere that comes and the spirit just hits you, and you lose control of yourself."** God words said: **"If they speak not according to this word, it is because there is not light in them."** (Isaiah 8:20) My friend, Michael Jackson spoke like a prophet. He claimed that he was sent forth to the world with a Message. But God's word warns: **"Beloved, believe not every spirit, but try the spirits whether they are of God: because many false prophets are gone out into the world."** (1 John 4:1) For Africa Columbia CBs Records 1985, Michael sang: "We are the world, we are the children. And all the different artistes joined together saying, we are the world, we are the children.

The **Lord Jesus Christ said the children of the world are the children of Satan, and the children of God are the children of light.** The song stated: "There comes a time when we need to heed a certain call and the world must come together as one." God's word warns: **That demonic spirits will bring the world together as one to fight against saints.** (Revelation 20: 7-15) The song goes on to say we are all part of God's great big family and the truth we know, love is all we need. The truth of the matter is, Jesus said: **"I am the way, the truth, and the life; no one cometh unto the Father, but by me"** (John 14:6). My friend to become a part of God's great big family, Jesus Christ said, **"Verily, verily, I say unto thee, except a man be born again, he cannot see the kingdom of God."** (John 3:3)

We cannot be God's children unless we are born again. Can you see the contradiction, in Michael Jackson's song? Michael Jackson, the Lord rebukes you! **This is a satanic deception that they can say that love is all we need, when**

they crucify love incarnate on the cross in the person of Jesus Christ and continue to reject him. Who they can fool? Not me! The song goes on to state: There's a choice we are making we are saving our own lives. But Jesus Christ said: **"For whosoever will save his life shall lose it: but whosoever will lose his life for my sake, the same save it."** (Luke 9:24) The song states: **As God has shown us by turning stones to bread and so we all must lend a helping hand.**

But Satan tempted Christ Jesus, Turn these stones into bread, but Jesus answered, "It is written, **Man shall not live by bread alone, but by every word that proceedeth out of the mouth of God."** (Matthew4:4) **The truth is that all of them are against Christ Jesus and his teachings.** My advice is that they must come to Jesus before it is too late. If Jesus had turned stones into bread when the Devil asked him to do so, he would have obeyed Satan and salvation would have been lost. Hence in Michael Jackson's song, there is wrong doctrine.

Madonna Pop singer

The most influential artist since the 80's has been Madonna. In the 80's and 90's into the 21st century she has also influenced millions of people through her music. **What's interesting is that she led many people through materialism—as being a material girl—and sexual promiscuity. Many of her lyrics conveyed a sexual looseness which led millions of children into being indiscreet in their dressing.** Some of them wanted to act and look like Madonna. But in 1990, **she switched from materialism into spiritualism—into the occult—which led them into the world of demonic.** Madonna is actually a siren. **A siren is a person who dresses like a Lolita to attract men to their death.** She is a siren used by Satan to drive people to hell—the lake of fire.

My friend, should we follow Madonna down to hell, or follow Jesus Christ, to heaven? God's word said: **"How art thou fallen from heaven, O Lucifer, son of the morning! How art thou cut down to the ground, which didst weaken the nations!"** (Isaiah 14:12-15) Should we follow Madonna and Lucifer, down to hell or the pit? **Madonna has admitted "I'm a tormented person. My pain is as big as, my joy. I have a lot of demons inside of me."** Do you know who is the tormented one? Yes, Satan, so you can hear by Madonna's confession that she is demon-possessed and under the influence of Satan's power. **Should you trust Madonna, or Lucifer?**(Matthew 4:5-11; John 8:44-45)

Madonna sings: "If I could melt your heart." Will you give such an evil person your heart? **Madonna told Rolling Stone about her company Siren Films,** "You know what a siren is, do you? A woman who draws men to their death, Madonna sings: "Give your-self to me." Read what (Proverbs 7:6-27) **Sirens were said to be nymphs who seduced sailors on passing ships through their singing and led them to destruction.** That is Satan's work, to lead people to destruction. **Pop artist Madonna**

uses her videos as a weapon to desensitize and demoralize her millions of fans into accepting the destructive practices of sexual immorality as normative.

God's word warns us: Avoid immorality. "Flee fornication. Every sin that a man commits is without the body; but he that committeth fornication sinneth against his own body." (1 Corinthians 6:18) My friend, God said: For the commandment is a lamp and the teaching is light . . . to keep you from the evil woman, from the smooth tongue of an adulteress. **Don't desire her beauty in your heart, nor let her catch you with her eyelids . . .** An adulteress hunts for the precious life. "Can a man take fire in his bosom and his clothes not be burned?" **"Whoever touches her will not go unpunished . . . The one who commits adultery with a woman is lacking sense; he who would destroy himself does it . . ."** She now sings: "If I could melt you heart."

Do not let your heart turn aside to her ways; do not stray into her paths. For many are the victims she has cast down, numerous are all her slain. Her house is the way to Hell and the chamber of hell descending to the chambers of death. **Madonna sings exposing her body and portrays a negative, whoring attitude towards life and boys.** For some, their public life might seem glamorous and perfect but what's in their private lives? They do not follow Gods principles: The Bible said: **"Every tree bringeth not forth good fruit is hewn down, and cast into the fire."** Help me cut her down.

(Proverbs 5:7; Matthew 7:17-19) **Madonna, through her elaborate infomercials promotes sexual immorality.**

She has helped to plunge untold millions into sexually transmitted diseases, and the destruction of hell. Should we listen to her while she is helping Satan kill mankind? Do not let her music-videos influence you, in doing evil. God's word warns: **Instead, you yourselves wrong and defraud one another, even your own brothers!** Surely you know that the wicked will not possess God's Kingdom. Do not fool yourselves; people who are immoral or who worship idols or are adulterers, homosexual perverts, who steal, who are greedy, drunkards, who slander others, or, who are thieves-none of these will possess God's Kingdom. (1 Corinthians 6:8-10)

These, Music Have Evil Forces Behind It!

My friend, when YOU listen to worldly music it is more than just enjoyment of beats and lyrics, for there are spirits behind it. **We can't see it in the musician but the music convey evil spirits that try to influence us into worshipping idols of sex, infatuation, lust, revenge, hate, anger and the many other things about which the artist sings or raps.** To withstand the hostile environment of music and its evil influences, you have to take a stand. When the enemies come in like a flood, the Spirit of the Lord shall lift up a standard against him (Isaiah 59:19). **That means, whatever plans Satan may have through**

music against you, if your standard is the same as God's, you will not be affected.

When you are in a taxi, maxi, or on the streets, and the music is playing, it will not have any effect on you. If you call on Jesus he will help you and deliver you from the snares of the enemy. **To call on him, just pray in your heart and mind. You will get through no matter what the Devil puts into your thoughts.** My friend, not all music is good for you. Some so-called Christian music is influenced by worldly beats and ambitions. **To learn more, get the book called "Reveling the truth about, Rock and Roll, Hip-Hop, Rap, Pop, Chutney, Soca and Dancehall."**

Look at lyrics and if they're not lining up with God's will don't listen to the music, even if your friends want you to. If you do listen to it, the spirits will get an opportunity to influence you. **Remember good music doesn't promote sex, homosexually, lust, drugs, violence, disobedience of the laws of the land or of your parents. It should be about motivation, and glorify God only.** I pray that God will influence your soul. Speak to God about it. Christians, keep Holy. Love all in Jesus Christ.

Madonna sings: "If I could melt your heart." Recent research studies have shown that the percentage of 15-year-olds who have had sex has skyrocketed from 10%, during the 60's sexual revolution, to over 50% today. **By the age of nineteen, 75% of our youths will have lost their virginity, and over 1million young ladies will have gotten pregnant before they finished high school.** Over one hundred thousand of them will kill their children every year. God would warn' us: "Marriage is honorable in all, and the bed undefiled: but whoremongers and adulterers God will judge." (Hebrews 13:4)

Nearly 40% of sexually active young people will contract one or more sexually transmitted diseases, including the deadly AIDS, and Human Papilloma Virus. In 1985, Madonna told Spin magazine: "Crucifixes are sexy because there's a naked man on them. **She also blasphemed Christ by saying "I think they probably got it on, Jesus and Mary Magdalene."** Madonna also practices her **Sarandon on women.** Madonna uses her videos as a weapon to desensitize and demoralize her millions of fans into accepting the destructive practices of homosexuality as normative.

My friend, you can see Satan is using Madonna, as an idol to influence people into practicing homosexuality, so should we listen to her music? Madonna admitted to a pro-homosexual magazine about her use of this technique as a means to deceive the masses. Who is the deceiver? Satan is. Madonna said: "They digest it on a lot of different levels. **Some people will see it and be disgusted by it, but maybe they'll be unconsciously aroused by it. If people keep seeing it and seeing it and seeing it, eventually it's not going to be** such a strange thing." (The Advocate, May7, 1991, Pg.4) The media will be used as a tool to deceive the masses.

God's word warns: "Wherefore God also gave them up to uncleanness through the lusts own hearts, to dishonor their own bodies between themselves: who exchanged the truth of God into a lie." (Romans 1:23-37; 32) Pop singer, Madonna also promotes sadomasochism. If Madonna admits to promoting homosexuality by showing herself with other women, what is she suggesting then? She said: **"Express yourself. Don't Repress yourself. Express yourself. Don't Repress yourself."** Should you listen to Madonna? This is ridiculous. You don't have to express yourself in homosexuality. There are other ways of expressing oneself without having to end up in the lake of fire. **She is telling you to disobey God's will, by expressing yourself and not repressing yourself.**

God's word declares: No man is to have sexual relations with another man or woman with woman; God hates that. He added: **"Thou shalt not lie with mankind, as with womankind: it is abomination. Neither shalt thou lie with any beast to defile thyself therewith: neither shall any woman stand before a beast to lie down thereto: it is confusion."** (Leviticus 18:22-34) My friend, why not listen to God? **The pentagram within a circle is one of the most common symbols in Satanism.**

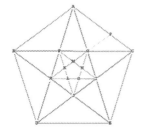

Madonna is listed as a "Role model" in the first church of Satan. Madonna also uses repetition, crowd participation and peer pressure to persuade and influence her audiences. And just what is Madonna teaching her massive fan base? Madonna brings her **"Sirendom"** to a culmination by leading her fans into a chant of going to Lake of FIRE! **Don't get entangled in her webs my friend.** She is teaching, and misleading in her singing. She said: **"I don't give a [expletive] and I don't give blame if I go to HELL!"** She tells her fans to repeat that statement. Isn't it foolish and irrational to allow this siren to lead you into the eternal fire?

Madonna knows what God's word says about the future of the wicked and will even quote from the book of Revelation 21: 8: **"The fearful, and unbelieving, and the abominable, and murderers, and whoremogers, and sorcerers, and idolaters, and all liars, shall have their part in the lake which burneth with fire and brimstone: which is the second death."** Madonna, gods and mortals in classical mythology states: **"The sirens were said to sing prophecies relating to the kingdom of Hades [hell]."** Nevertheless, God has shown us how to stop Satan influence upon us which has us sinning, Satan is killing us. **God has shown us <u>because</u> He is not going to stop Satan for us.**

Rather, He shows us in the New Testament a greater power than Satan's power. **He shows us how to get this power and use it against Satan and his music ministers worldwide.** The power that I am speaking of is the **HOLY SPIRIT POWER.** From these Scriptures it is clear that Jesus came to destroy the works of Satan and his influences and He is sending us to do the same works.

I believe that the "greater works" is stopping the music today that are influencing millions of people worldwide, the music is teaching them to kill human beings; and disobey, and dress like Lolita, and have illicit sexual relationships including homosexuality. My friend, it cannot be stopped by laws or guns. Jesus gave us Christians the power, by the Holy Spirit. Listen! **"Behold, I give you power to tread on serpents and scorpions, and over all the power of the enemy: and nothing shall by any means hurt you."** (Luke 10:19)

To Stop The Ungodly Musical Influence On Humans, You Must Do These Three Things:

1 Invite the Holy Spirit into your life by receiving Jesus as your personal Savior. 2 Receive the anointing and power of the Holy Spirit so you can destroy the works of Satan influences. Use the name of Jesus to break curses of ungodly music influence. **3. Select Powerful Scriptures and quote them <u>distinctly</u> to Satan.** These power Scriptures include: Luke 10:19; Acts 1:8;

and Mark 16:17-18. **With thousands of us following these steps, we'll break the curses and influence that Satan and his men have upon us. We can do this together, in Jesus name!**

Many folks say that whenever you feel sad, just listen to a Dancehall, or a Soca music. That is deception, that is what Satan is using against us today. **You know something, you do that, it works for a while and afterwards you become sad again. It is more like a smoker, who has problems at home, so he leaves and goes to a pub to smoke, in an effort to forget his problems at home.** Is his problem gone? **No. Well, these Dancehall and Soca music is just like that.** It appears to be gone, but it is still there. Jesus can help with your sadness! **Everything you ask for in prayer will be yours, if you only have faith**Mark11:24)

When you feel worried, hurt, sad, or angry, you don't have to listen to a Dancehall nor Soca. Don't allow Satan to destroy you, please. Hear what God's word says: **"Casting all your care upon him; for he careth for you."** God warned us, "Be sober, be vigilant; because your adversary the devil, as a roaring lion, walketh about, seeking whom he may devour." (1 Peter 5:7-9)

CHAPTER 14

Is Abortion Right?

This generation is being made to believe that abortion is not only right, but also a right for every woman. Very few are saying that it is not wrong to have an abortion. **What does God say, about it?** He said it is wrong! I will tell a story about a man called Marcus. **Marcus had grown up to believe that abortion was a serious sin, tantamount to murder.** His girlfriend, Angel became pregnant and Marcus could not face the consequences of commitment and parenthood. He quickly opted for the convenient solution: Marcus told Angel that she had to have an abortion, because he did not want the expenses of commitment. **My friend, is this a right DECISION?**

Angel answered her boyfriend, "In my heart I feel it is wrong; we've already committed a sin, so why should we sin again by way of murder?" She told Marcus, that she will not have an abortion because it is wrong. What Marcus called a convenient solution to an unplanned and unwanted pregnancy is not uncommon. The 2007 global study reported that in 2003 there were an estimated 42million induced abortions: from every race and nationality, from a variety of religious backgrounds, and from every level of income, education, from puberty to middle age.

The cup of sin is overflowing. Do not add to the number of abortion murders. Think before you act! Angel said, "It felt like there was a life inside of me. I realized that if I stayed with Marcus, he would not support me during my pregnancy, but I held on to God's word" "Casting all your cares upon him; for he careth for you." (1 Peter 5:7) She said by keeping faith in God's word, Marcus later altered his thinking and asked her to marry him. Marcus said, "We have no car, nor money, a few clothes and very little of everything." But Angel encouraged him, have faith in God, because His words are true.

"But seek ye first the Kingdom of God, and his righteousness' and all these things shall be added unto you." (Matthew 6:33) My friend, Proverbs 21:5 said: "Plan carefully and you will have plenty; if you act too quickly, you will never have enough." Words of advice: It is dangerous to

be concerned with what others think of you, but if you trust the LORD, you are safe. (Proverbs 29:25) This Scripture is very important, please read Psalm 25:14! Well, if you were facing an unwanted pregnancy, how would you deal with such a situation? Why do so many people choose abortion?

They do so for a variety of reasons, ranging from financial problems to perhaps abusive relationship that result in their not wanting any further ties with the man or woman. **Sometimes, the pregnancy may simply not fit into the plans of the woman or the couple. There are also times when abortion is chosen to protect someone's reputation. This is a common secret of an abortion**: One woman who was seeking an abortion confessed: "My parents are very religious . . . . If I had a baby out of wedlock; it would be a sin to them. Their friends would say to them that your daughter has sinned." **You know something, my friend, they would make fun of her and judge her saying she had sinned but how do they feel about abortion?**

The girl confided: "Oh, abortion. That is totally forgivable. But it is the lesser evil because it would be a secret. If I have an abortion, [My parents and pastor and friends in church will never know]. **But, God sees you, and he will judge you for such evil thought. It's sin!** Regardless of any situation, it is wrong in the eyes or your Creator to do or think such evil. Usually a pregnancy is often intensely painful. But is abortion a trouble-free solution? **Consider the consequences.**

Today many women who commit abortion cannot become pregnant again and struggle to forgive themselves. Since guilt is such a pervasive problem-even among those who do not consider themselves religious. Why do so many young women still have abortions? **They don't know what are the facts of life and death.**

Why We Did Not Have An Abortion

There was a seventeen-year-old, Christian girl named Roma, who became pregnant by her boyfriend just as she was about to start business school. **Her mother, a widow with seven children, was devastated.** She had wanted her daughter to learn a trade so she could rise out of their poverty. **In desperation the mother insisted that Roma have an abortion.** When the doctor asked her if she wanted to go through with the abortion, Roma explained, "I told him No!" Bewildered at seeing Roma's promising future disappear and contemplating the stress of another child, her mother forced her to leave home. **Roma was able to stay with her aunt.** A few weeks later, her mother realized it was the right thing to keep the child and allowed her to return home to have her grandchild. **Roma's mother helped her to care for Mark, her grandson and she has grown to love the little boy intensely.**

Friendship with God has Power

The Bible states: "The secret of the LORD is with them that fear him; and he will shew them his covenant." (Psalm 25:14) What influences the decision of many who refuse to have an abortion is their consideration for how their Creator feels about the matter. **Enjoying friendship with God is doing what pleases him.** God is their paramount concern. **This concern is what strongly influenced my firm belief that God gives life, and No one has the right to take the life he had given to them.** When Roma began to study the Bible, her friendship with God grew. She noted that making the right decision to keep her child caused her to feel much closer to God and made her want to please him in all aspects of my life. She continued, **"When I prayed for his direction, everything else just fell into place."**

Roma, refused an abortion despite of her mother unkindness "Two weeks after my son's birth," She reports, I was contacted by the Holy Spirit and learned how to bring my life into full harmony with God's laws. **I soon began to teach my son the value of obeying God, and over time he developed a strong love for God he is now a pastor.** God loves him, same as me. Reflecting on what his mother did, Mark said: **"Knowing that she had so much love for me that she allowed me to live despite the circumstances she was under, motivated me to use my life in the best way I could to show my appreciation to God for this wonderful gift—life,"**

So I advise you, **my friend, please don't take an abortion. If you have a child out of marriage, it is evidence of the sin of fornication.** The best things to do is to repent of that sin (fornication), NOT TO HAVE AN ABORTION! Don't let it happen again. **If someone wants to judge you for having a child out of marriage, tell them, "Yes, I have sinned, and now I am doing the right thing, by keeping my child."** Many who have come to understand God's view of life have no regrets for their decision to preserve the life of the child they now treasure. They can say from their hearts' brimming with gratitude, "We did not have an abortion!"

God Bless You! **Friendship with God, the source of life deepens on your respect for the life in the womb.** The Scriptures said: God is the source of all life, and because of your light, we see the light. (Psalm 36:9) God can help you with his supreme **Power beyond what is normal to help you cope with any unplanned pregnancy.** (2 Corinthians 4:7) Looking back at those who showed respect for God's view of life: **How do you feel about their decision?** Well I feel blessed to know that there are people who do the right thing still. How do you feel?

1 ....

2 ....

3 ....

No Regrets!

These parents are not plagued by feelings of guilt or any unresolved sense of sadness and loss. **In time, they truly view 'the fruitage of the belly' as a reward, not a curse!** Psalm 127:3 said: **"Lo, children are an heritage of the LORD: and the fruit of the womb is his reward."** Just a few hours after giving birth, Roma excitedly, she called her workmate and told her how thrilled she was with the prospect of rearing her little boy. **Bursting with joy, she added: "It is so true that God blesses those who do what pleases him."**

Why is acting in harmony with God's view of life so beneficial? Because as the source of life, God says obey all his laws. I am giving them to you today for your benefit. (Deuteronomy 10:13) **My advice to you is: No matter what circumstances you are in, do not have an abortion, just have faith in Jesus Christ, and I promise you that everything will be all right!** And for those who do not have Jesus, get him, he can work for you too. One more thing, do not have sex out of marriage. **Prepare yourself financially so that you can get married when you meet the person God has for you! Remember always be prepared and you will prosper.**

Abortion

When does life begin? See this Bible text for your answer. (Psalm 51:5) **What is the value of an unborn child?** (Psalm

139:13-16; Jeremiah 1:5) **Is abortion absolutely wrong?** (Genesis 9:5-6) **Murder is forbidden.** (Proverbs 24:11-12) **Can I be forgiven if I have had an abortion or encouraged someone else to have one?** (Isaiah1:18; Psalm 103:3; 1 John 1:9) **PROMISE FROM GOD:** (Jeremiah 1:5)—I knew you before I formed you in your mother's womb. Read some more Holy Scriptures: (Psalm 25:14-16; Ecclesiastes 7:1-7)

CHAPTER 15

Church, a Godly View of Life!

Today In our day many folks show no value for life; no respect; their hearts are cold, and for this God is angry. As Prophet Jeremiah said: **"But the LORD is the true God, he is the living God, and an everlasting king: at his wrath the earth shall tremble, and the nation shall not be able to abide his indignation."** (Jeremiah 10:10) "Thou art worthy, O Lord, to receive glory, honor, and power: for thou hast created all things, and for you pleasure they are and were created." (Revelation 4:11) King David sings and praises God: **"For with thee is the fountain of life: in thy light shall we see light."** (Psalm 36:9) Therefore, my friend, life is a gift from God, and it should be valued, so, respect life!

How Do You Show Respect for Life?

God's word has declared, 'For In him we live, and move, and have our being; as certain also of your own poets have said, for we are his offspring. He provides the food you eat, the water you drink, the air you breathe, and the land you live on." (Acts 17:28; Acts 14:15-17) In this way God has made life enjoyable. But to enjoy life to the fullest, you need to learn and obey God's laws. (Isaiah 48:17-18) God wants you to have respect for life: both your own and that of others. Adam and Eve's son, Cain became very angry with his brother, Abel.

God warned Cain that his anger could lead him to sin. Cain ignored that warning. Cain killed his brother, Abel. (Genesis 4:3-8) God punished Cain for murdering his brother, Abel. (Genesis 4:9-11)

My friend, to truly respect one's life, one must do as the Bible says: "Thou shalt love thy neighbor as thyself." Unconditionally! "Thou shalt Love the LORD thy God with all thy heart, and with all thy soul, and with all thy mind." (Matthew 22:37-39; Luke 3:8-11) Obedience of these two great commands will confirm that you are a child of God who values life. To Love your neighbour as yourself, you must do for others what you would want them to do for you. Thousands of years ago, God gave the people of Israel laws to help them to serve him acceptably. The laws were given through the prophet, Moses. One of the laws of Moses said: **"Thou shalt not kill."** (Deuteronomy 5:17) This showed that God values human life and that people must value the lives of others.

How Does God View Abortion?

My friend, what about the life of an unborn child? Well, according to the Law of Moses, causing the death of a body in its mother's womb was wrong. Yes even such a life is precious to God. **This means that abortion is wrong, and God will judge anyone who takes an abortion.** (Exodus 21:22-23; Psalm 127: 3) Having respect for life includes having right view for human life. The Bible says: **"Whoever hates his brother is a murderer, and you know that a murderer does not have eternal life abiding in him."** (1 John 3:15) God also said: "We should love one another." (1 John 3:11-12)

It is vital that you view life and learn to love one another unconditionally. What about showing respect for your own life? People normally do not want to die, but some risk death for the sake of pleasure. **Many, for example, use tobacco, chew betel nut, take drugs for recreational purposes, or even sleep with one another. Such substances harm the body and often kill the users. A person who makes a practice of using these substances does not view life as sacred.** These practices are unclean in God's eyes. (2 Corinthians 7: 1-4; Romans 6:19; 12:12)

To serve God with righteousness one has to give up such practices although doing so might be very hard, God can give us the necessary help and he appreciates the effort we make to treat our lives as a precious gift from him. If you have respect for life, you will carefully monitor your health and safety. **You will not be careless and will not take risks just for pleasure or excitement.** My friend, you will avoid reckless driving and violent or dangerous sports. (Psalm 11: 5) God's law for ancient Israel stated: **'When you build a new house, be sure to put a railing around the edge of the roof.**

Then you will not be responsible if someone falls off and die.' (Deuteronomy 22:8) **In harmony with the principle set out in that law, keep such things as stairs in good condition in your home so that someone does not trip, fall, and get badly hurt. If you own a bus or a car make sure that it is safe to drive.** Do not let either your home or your bus or car be a danger to you or to others. Thank you! **To recap everything, life is a gift from God.** (Psalm 36:9; Revelation 4:11). Abortion is wrong since the life of an unborn child is precious in God's eyes.

Have value for life my friend. (Exodus 21:22-23; Psalm 127:3)

CHAPTER 16

What Is the Worship That God Approves?
Are all religions pleasing to God?

There are, hundreds of religions that claim to teach the truth about God. Yet, their teachings are different. If there is one God, why are there so much different teachings? There must be false gods as well as religions. **How can you know the right way to worship God? Some say you have to study and compare the teachings of many religions, is that true? No,** my friend, you need only to learn what the Bible really teaches about true worship. To demonstrate: In many lands, there is a problem with counterfeit money.

If you were given the job to pick out such false money, how would you go about doing it? Is it by memorizing every kind of money? No! Your time would be better spent if you studied real money. When you know what real money looked like, you could recognize a counterfeit. **So, my friend, learn the Bible and you will know false teachings!**

How Can You Identify The True Religion?

How do we identify true religion and recognize those religions that are false? **It is important that we worship God in the way that he approves—in Spirit and in Truth.** Many people believe that all religions are pleasing to God, but the Bible does not teach that. It is not even enough just to be a Christian. For example Jesus said: **"Not everyone that saith unto me, Lord, Lord, shall enter into the kingdom of Heaven; but he that doeth the will of my Father which is in heaven."** To have God's approval, therefore, you must learn what God requires of you and do it. Jesus called those who did not do God's will, wicked, or lawless people. (Matthew 7:21-23)

Counterfeit money has no real value. Likewise, false religions are actually harmful to us. God gives everyone on earth the opportunity to gain everlasting life. To obtain eternal life, you must worship God properly and live in a way that is acceptable to him. Sadly, many refuse to do so! **One person may say: "It doesn't matter, which path one takes; all roads lead to the same God." To prove that false religions are out there, such statements are being regularly made.** Jesus also talked about two roads He said: "Enter ye in at the strait gate: for wide is the gate, and broad is the way, that leadeth to destruction, and many there be which go in thereat: because strait is the gate, and narrow is the way, which leadeth unto life, and few there be that find it." (Matthew 7:13-14)

Therefore true religion leads to everlasting life, but false religion leads to the lake of fire and destruction. So, my friend, don't accept everything you hear someone says. Remember there are many false religions and teachings. Read the Bible to know the truth. **The Lord is not slow to do what he has promised, as some think. Instead, he is patient with you, because God does not want any human to be destroyed and go to the lake of fire.** God wants all to turn away from their sins, therefore he is giving people everywhere an opportunity to learn about him. (Matthew 25:41; 2 Peter 3:9)

So grasp the opportunity, my friend! It really matters how we worship God. This may mean either life or death for us. The true religion is evident in the lives of the people who practise it. By their fruits you shall recognize them. Jesus said: **"Ye shall know them by their fruits. Do men gather grapes of thorns, or figs of thistles? Even so, every good tree bringeth forth good fruit; but a corrupt tree bringeth forth evil fruit. A good tree cannot bring forth evil fruit, neither can a corrupt tree bring forth good fruit."** Every tree that bringeth not forth good fruit is hewn down, and cast into the fire." **This means that false religions should be rejected!** (Matthew 7:16-19)

In other words, those who practise true religion would be recognized by their fruit and their conduct. True worshippers, as a group, seek to do God's will. Let us consider some that identify with the practice of the true religion.

Who Are God's True Worshipers on Earth Today?

My friend, God's true servants base their teachings on the Bible. "All Scriptures are given by inspiration of God, and is profitable for doctrine, for reproof, for correction, for instruction in righteousness: that the man of God may be perfect, thoroughly furnished unto all good works." (2 Timothy 3:16-17) To his fellow Christians, the apostle Paul wrote: **"For this cause also thank we God without ceasing, because, when ye received it not as the word of men, but as it is in truth, the word of God, which effectually worketh also in you that believe."** (1 Thessalonians 2:13). God is at work in the lives of everyone who believes it. True servants of God do not base their faith on human views or tradition, such as the trinity doctrine, money, or blessing. **Their faith originates from God's inspired word, the Bible, and rejects all errors!**

Jesus Christ set his example based on God's teachings. He prays to his Heavenly Father, he said "your word is true." (John 17: 17) **Jesus believed the word of God and everything he taught harmonized with the Scriptures.** Jesus often said: It is written. God's people today do not teach their own ideas.

They believe that the Bible is God's Word and they base their teachings firmly on what it says. **Those who practice the true religion worship only God and show unconditional love to all. Jesus declared that it is the Most High God you must worship and serve only him!** (Matthew 4:10) Thus, God's servants worship no one other than God (I Am). The Supreme ruler over all the earth; he is the Most High God.

Jesus set the pattern in helping others to get to know God as he said in prayer: I have manifested your name that you have given me, out of the world. (John 17:6) **True worshippers today teach others about God's Kingdom.** God's people show genuine, unselfish love for one another. Jesus said: **"By this shall all men know that ye are my disciples, if ye have love one to another."** (John 13: 35) The early Christians had such love for one another. Godly love for all these qualities binds all things together in perfect unity. (Colossians 3:14) **Members of false religions do not have such brotherly love. How do we know that?** They kill one another because of national or ethnic differences. True Christians do not take up weapons to kill or harm their Christian brother or anyone else.

The Bible states: **"In this the children of God's are manifest, and the children of the devil: whosoever doeth not righteousness is not of God, neither he that loveth not.** Ye heard from the beginning, that we should love one another. Not as **Cain, who was of that wicked one, and his brother. And wherefore slew he him? Because his own works were** evil, and his brother's righteous." (1 John 3:10-12) Today, people act this way, having no love for one another. **My friend, don't be like them, but love one another.** The Bible says: "If a man say, I love God, and hateth his brother, he is a liar: for he that loveth not his brother whom he hath seen, how can he love God whom he hath not seen?" The command that Christ has given us is this: **"Whoever loves God must love his brother also."** (1 John 4:20-21)

Of course, genuine love means more than not killing others. True Christians, let us continue to love others and to help one another, under all circumstances. Let us encourage one another since you understand that the Day of the Lord is near. (Hebrews10:24-25) So then, as often as you have the chance, you should do well to everyone, and especially to those who belong to your family in the faith. (Galatians 6:10) True Christians accept Jesus Christ as God. The Bible says: **"Neither is there salvation in any other: for there is none other name under heaven given among men, whereby we must be saved."** (Acts 4:12); (Matthew 20:28). In addition, Jesus is God's appointed King in the Heavenly Kingdom that will rule the entire earth. God requires that you obey Jesus and apply his teachings, if you want everlasting life.

That is why the Bible states: **"He that believeth on the Son hath everlasting life: and he that believeth not the Son shall not see life; but the wrath of God abideth on him."** (John 3:36). My friend, true worshippers are not part of the world, and this can be proven. When on trial before the Roman ruler Pilate, Jesus said: **"My kingdom does not belong to this world."** (John 18:36) Regardless of which country they live in, Jesus' true followers are subjects of his Heavenly Kingdom and maintain strict neutrality in the world's political affairs. They take no part in its conflicts. **God's true worshippers respect the rights of individuals. They are free to choose a political party, run for office, or vote.**

Where there is a conflict between what God requires and what a political system requires, true worshipers follow the example of the apostles, who said: We must obey God, as ruler, rather than men, that means obey God not men. (Acts 5:29; Mark 12:17) **Jesus' true followers preach that God's kingdom is mankind's only hope.** Jesus foretold: "And this gospel of the Kingdom shall be preached in all the world for a witness unto all nation; and then shall the end come." (Matthew 24:14) Instead of encouraging aging people to look to human rulers to solve their problems, **true followers of Jesus Christ proclaim God's Heavenly Kingdom as the only hope for mankind.** (Psalm 146:3-4)

My friend, on the basis of what you have just considered, ask yourself: Which religious groups' teachings are based on the Bible or promote God's will? Which group practises Godly love and exercises faith in Jesus? **Which religion renounces the love of the world, and proclaims that God's kingdom is the only real hope for mankind? Of all the religious groups** on earth, which one meets all these requirements? (1 John 1-21) Simply believing in God is not enough to please him. Do you believe that there is only one God? Yes! (1 Corinthians 8:6) The demons also believe and tremble with fear. (James 2:19) Obviously though, they do not do God's will and do not have the approval of God. **My friend, to be approved by God, not only must you believe in his existence but you must also do his will, you must also break free from false religions and embrace true worship.**

The Bible showed that you must not take any part in false worship. It said: You must leave them and separate yourself from them. Have nothing to do with what is unclean. **True Christians therefore would avoid anything that is connected with false worship.** (2 Corinthians 6:17; Isaiah 52:11) The Bible shows that all of the many forms of false religions are part of Babylon the great. (Revelation 17:5) **"The Lord is not slack concerning his promise, as some men count slackness; but is longsuffering to us-ward, not willing that any should perish, but that all should come to repentance."** (2 Peter 3:9-13)

What a marvelous world that will be! And in the righteous new system, there will be only one religion and one, true worship. **Is it not the course of wisdom for you to take the necessary steps to come into association with true worshippers right now?** God loves you and He wants you to get wisdom. Read and understand, one love! **My advice to you** is to keep the faith, proclaim God's word, and, no matter what the circumstance, demonstrate your unconditional love. By this you will be certified a true worshipper of God! Moreover, you will be empowered to identify falsehood when it comes to you. One Love!

CHAPTER 17

How Can I Have Confidence In Myself?

Most youths, and even older folks, struggle with low self-esteem and lack of self-confidence in their appearance, their abilities, as well as how they measure up to others. **Some girls even go with boys and engage in sexual activities to make themselves feel beautiful and gain acceptance! If you fall into that category, help is on the way.** My friend, you have a problem! Many people say, "My imperfections cause me to feel down. Usually, I am my own worst critic." **No matter how beautiful or handsome you are, you will always come across others who are 'better-looking.'**

My friend, **true beauty consists of your true inner self, the ageless beauty of a gentle and quiet spirit, which is of the**

greatest value in God's sight. (1 Peter 3:4) Rondell said: "I get very self-conscious around others. I'm scared that I'll look like a loser." You can get help with the wisdom which the Bible contains. **Consider the virtue of self-respect. That will help you to see or identify yourself in a more positive light.**

1. Make Friends

It is written, **"A friend loveth at all time, and a brother is born for adversity."** (Proverbs 17:17) This means that a good friend can be a tremendous support during times of adversity or troubles. Friends can protect you and say something that would help and encourage you. (1 Samuel 18:1; 19:2) **Draw close to those who have a positive influence on your life. Even the thought that someone cares can lift your spirit.** (1 Corinthian 16:17-18)

Sometimes the most important thing is knowing that someone really sincerely cares for you. I know it can make you feel absolutely confident and valuable about yourself. God is the biggest friend you will ever have. He loves you, and wants the best for you. Why? **It's because he shaped and molded you in your mother's womb. He knows the number of hair you have on your head.** He designed you precisely to fulfill your purpose, and most important of all, he finds good things to say about you. The Bible is a love story for you, so just read! God himself said he loves you: **"I am fearfully and wonderfully** made: marvellous are thy works; and that my soul knoweth right well." (Psalms 139:14)

2. Get Wisdom

My friend, Keep Company with the wise and you will become wise. If you make friends with foolish people, you will be ruined. Ensure that your friends bring out the real you, and not a person that they created just to fit in. (Proverbs 13:20) **"Do not be deceived: Evil communication corrupt good manners."** (1 Corinthians 15:33) Engaging in unwise act just to impress others will leave you feeling degraded and used. **Hear what God have to say on this matter: "What did you gain from doing the things that you are now ashamed of? Nothing! The result of those things is death!"** (Romans 6:21)

You don't have to do immoral things to feel good, about yourself; don't let anyone tell you that, that is a lie! And if they were your friends, they would want the best for you at all times. **Only those who love you would tell you to do the right thing.** In addition they would not curse you, or put you down. If you have negative people around you, get away from them and create a positive mindset using the Bible. My friend, if you can work hard to improve your imperfection, then you should do it. **This also helps your self-esteem and self-actualization when you realize you can overcome anything.**

For example: Shanice was always terrible at math. It was so bad; it prevented her from moving up in her career. She was always self-conscious about it and was easily intimidated by others in her work place. **Finally, she decided to go back to school and face the fear of mathematics. She practiced and worked diligently at it.** When the results came for math, Shanice was astonished at her achievement. She was successful. This helped her to apply for a better job position and launched her career. It also boosted her confidence level. **Not to be forgotten, was the fact that every night Shanice would pray for guidance, and for focus on her school work.** This helped to increase her faith in God. Getting the wisdom to do things develops our self-confidence too.

3. Gain self Confidence, By Helping One Another!

My friend you must work hard in this way and help to elevate one another's confidence and self-respect remembering the words that the Lord Jesus himself said, "It is more blessed to give than to receive." (Acts 20:35) **When you help others, you help yourself. Be generous, and you will be prosperous. Help, others, and you will be helped."** (Proverbs 11:25). That does not include allowing someone to take advantage of you or letting them to have everything while you're left with nothing. It simply means to share and still have enough to live comfortably.

"I think of what I can do for others and try to fill a need for someone in my church. **Giving unconditional love and attention to others, and helping the needy makes me feel better,**" said Lurissa. "The Christian faith is rewarding because it forces you to stop thinking about yourself and start thinking about others" said Cheryl. Read. (Matthew 6:2-4) **Giving with the wrong motive falls flat. It is usually for others to see and for recognition this is the wrong motive.** (1 Thessalonians 2:5-6) When you give to others you will be blessed. It also helps people. It may even save someone's life or win them to Christ. **A gift is never too small; even the poor should give!**

When the poor widow gave her flour and oil to the prophet, she got more in return. This is a good example. It makes you feel good about yourself. This really helps take the mind off your imperfections and helps you focus on something bigger, like helping people. You would soon begin to see how irrelevant your imperfection becomes. For example, when Shanice started math, she also discovered that there were others who were weaker than she. **SHANICE NEVER THOUGHT SHE WOULD BE HELPING OTHERS WITH THAT SUBJECT.**

By God's grace, Shanice learnt to be helpful. The activity also stimulated her memory and contributed to her success. **This was a great way to help herself while helping others.** She found that it was very fulfilling to help others while considering yourself blessed, even in small things. **Contact me if you need** anything. **Was your confidence boosted up?** If so, email me at truthofsalvation463@ymail.com. Or add me to Skype, namely: jesusiscominyou. You can make your arrangement. I will end with this: Go to the Bible at (Proverbs 24:16): "**No matter how often an honest man falls, he always gets up again; but disaster destroys the wicked, so get up.**"

My advice!

Help one another; don't take advantage of helpless people. **My friend, when you take advantage of helpless people that results in low self-respect, and lack of confidence.** Instead, help motivate or boost them up, for this is the right thing to do. **Demonstrate your love in action: lift them up!**

CHAPTER 18

Immoral Dressing, What, I Can Wear?

Nowadays, it is very fashionable for young people to dress like Lolita; Lolita means to have a very sexual appearance and behave in a very sensual manner. This has to stop! **Is there any way to declare a solution?** Yes! I know the secret. You do not have to dress like a Lolita. **Does that mean you have to dress like an 84-year-old woman? It just means that you should be modest in your dressing, so you can gain the respect you deserve and you can be happy about yourself.** My friend, this will benefit you. When you will look like a Lolita, men will view you as a sex object. However when you dress modestly your peers, will say to you, "You dress respectfully, I love this about you."

Such words will being honor to you, wouldn't it? In this way no one can criticize what you wear. So my friend, let's get started. Think of a "wonderful" outfit that you like. **The first important thing to do is . . . . Consider Bible principles!** The Bible give some solution about dressing, in fact, you could read along all the Scriptural admonition that directly relates to the subject in just a couple of minutes! In that time, though, you would find valuable solutions or guide lines. For example: **The Bible advises a distinct, woman to be modest and sensible about her clothes and to dress properly.** (1Timothy 2:9-10) Dressing "Modestly" cannot cause you worry or pain.

In this context modesty means that your clothes should show self-respect and show consideration for others. **My friend, dressing ridiculously and horsier or Lolita, is unwise.** Don't let your body be unclean, but completely holy be living in awe of God. (2 Corinthians 6:3; 7:1) A wide variety of clothing fits those criteria. "It might be challenging," says Shanice, age 21, but you can be fashionable without wearing extreme, styles, Lolita. The Scripture says that when it comes to appearance, you should focus on your real beauty. In other words: **"A meek and quiet spirit, which is in the sight of God of great price."** Yes greatest value in God's sight. (1 Peter 3:4)

An immodest outfit may momentarily turn heads, but it's your inner beauty that will win the long-term respect of adults and your peers. Yes even they may see the folly of excessive styles. "It's disgusting to see the way women practically throw themselves at men by what they wear!" **Angela says: "everything she wear had 'look-at-me' and sex me' written all over it. She wanted the attention of the guys, and to get it she would wear the most eye-catching outfits she could find.** My friend, this says, guys will only look at you as a sex object. Warning: Avoid styles that highlight Lolita. It, makes you appear desperate and self-absorbed and ridiculous, you may think you look good, you may ask a guy, and he will say you look sexy, this is my point, a sex object.

Please, look up the meaning of sexy. **Dress like a Lolita, could also make you a target for harassment-or worse.** In fact modest clothing enhances your appearance and highlights your good qualities (individual), quality. My friend, 'it's all right to have style in what you wear, as long as it doesn't conflict with the Bible principles.' **There are a lot of things that you can buy that looks good and are not objectionable.** When I was a teenager, I wanted to be independent; I didn't like being told what I could wear. In time, though I realized that I wasn't getting the respect I wanted-not until I started considering the Bible opinion or principles. Lurissa said **"When I see girls wearing sleazy clothes, my respect for them decreases, on the other hand, when I see people wearing modest clothing, I say to myself, 'That's how I want people to see me."**

My friend, in this world there are so many girls that dress ridiculous and look like Lolita. If you were to confront them about it, the usual response would be, **"You are not my father,** or mother. **I am independent, and I can buy anything I want and dress any way I want.**" The truth is not even there father or mother could tell them anything. This is the wrong attitude to have. You need to develop respect for yourselves. **You know there are many pastors who see young women looking like Lolita, in other words a sex object (low self-respect).** But do you know what they do? Nothing—because they are afraid, because they will lose members in their church (money); what a pity!

My friend, modesty dressing is very good; you will get the respect you deserve. But if you don't dress modestly: **Such as wearing sleazy clothes your respect will disappear, just like a puff of smoke which appears for a moment and then disappears. So get started!** (James 4:14; 1 Peter 3:4-7) My friend, appreciate my advice; because I don't want you walk out of your house; embarrassing yourself and making others see you as a sex abject. **Or to be the one that people are talking about negatively because of your appearance.** Be modesty!

My friend, let's face it: As long as you are under Christ Jesus authority' [blood]. **Get all the advice you can, and you will succeed; without it you will fail. What a joy it is to find just the right word for the right occasion!** My friend, walk the road that leads upward, not the road that leads downward to death (Proverbs 15: 22-24) My friend, my words will benefit you, but you can kill yourself with stupidity. **Be quiet, it is foolish to enjoy doing wrong, or looking like a Lolita.**

"Intelligent people take pleasure in advice, and wisdom."
(Proverbs 10:20-23)

Modesty, My friend!

What is the importance of modesty? Read these Bible texts
for your answers.
(1Timothy 2:15; 1 Peter 3:1-2)

How can I be modest in my appearance? (1 Corinthians 6:19;
1 Timothy 2:9; 1 Peter 3:3-4)

How can I show modesty in my behaviour? (Romans 13:13;
Ephesians 5:8; Titus 2:12)

PROMISE FROM GOD: (1Peter 2:12) Be careful how you
live among your unbelieving neighbors. **Even if they accuse
you of doing wrong, they will see your honorable behavior,
and they will believe and give honor to God when he comes
to judge the world.**

Thank you! **Consider obeying God's will, for it will save
your life.** I know God can still help you, just let Him. **Being
modest is not bad, but it gives you respect; not only respect,
but people will see you as a decent and well-mannered and a
respectable person.** Do you want people to see you like this?
Yes, so then be modest.

CHAPTER 19

Will Sex Improve Your Relationship?

There are many people who think that having sex will improve their relationship, so, when they fall out, they have intercourse and make up. Do you think this addresses the problem? **It is just like a smoker who has problems at home and goes out the road and takes a smoke, but the truth is, the problem is still there. So this is a false perception!** Find your problem, get a solution, and you will not have to have sex, to make it right, or smoke, because it will not help. **Cowards run, my friend find the problem and fix it!** I will tell you a story about a man called Lewis, and his girlfriend, Adriane. Adriane had been seeing Lewis for only two months, but she felt as if she had known him forever.

They texted each other and talked on the phone for several hours each day. Adriane wanted more than conversation during the two months. Lewis and Adriane had done nothing more than hold hands and briefly kiss. Lewis didn't want to go any further, but he doesn't want to lose her either. No one made her feel so worthy, or so special. Besides, Lewis and Adriane were in love. My friend you probably guess where the scenario is heading. But what you may not realize is how dramatically sex would have changed things for Lewis and Adriane; and not for the better. I am talking from experience. **Consider if you want to have sex out of marriage, you will suffer the consequences.**

That is true if you disrespect the law, such as the one that states: that you should abstain from fornication. You will be punished, my friend. God wants you to be holy and completely free from sexual immorality. (1 Thessalonians 4:3) **What are the consequences of disobeying that command?** One: "He who is guilty of fornication and sexual immorality is sinning against his own body." (1 Corinthians 6:18) How is that true? See if you can list below three (3) harmful effects that can come to those who engage in premarital sex.

1 ....

2 ....

3 ....

Now, my friend, look at what you wrote. **Did you include such things as sexually transmitted diseases, unwanted pregnancy, or the loss of God's favor?** Can you see the consequences that can come to anyone who violates God's law regarding fornication or immorality? **Nevertheless, you might be tempted.** You may say, "Nothing will happen to me, I could reason. After all, everyone is having sex". **You will even feel that sex will bring you and your partner closer. Yes!**

Sex is when a man and a woman become close in a very special way, but only under one circumstance, marriage. God only wants a man and a woman who are married to each other to have sexual relations. Besides, who wants to be ridiculed for being a virgin? Isn't it better to give in? Not at all! Not so fast! **Keep your virginity for your husband, do not let anyone ridicule you, and tell them what God said about sex before marriage.** (1 Corinthians 6:9-20)

(1)   Distress. Most youths who have engaged in premarital sex say that they regretted it afterward.

(2)   Distrust. After having sex, each partner begins to wonder, "Who else has he\she had sex with?"

(3)   Disloyalty. After having sex, a boy is more likely to dump his girlfriend and move on to someone else.

(4)   Disillusionment. Deep down, a girl would have preferred someone who would protect her and not use her, for sex. In addition, consider' this:

Many boys have said that they would never marry a girl with whom they have had sex. Why? Because they'd prefer someone who is more chaste! Does that surprise you—perhaps even angered you? If so, whether you are a girl or a boy, remember this: **The reality of premarital sex is far different from what is shown in movies and on TV. The entertainment industry glamorizes teen sex and makes it look like true love.** That is false! Don't be naïve! Those who would try to coax you into premarital sex are only looking after their own interests. **If your boyfriend or girlfriend, loves you unconditionally, they will manifest this: "Charity suffereth long, and is kind; charity envieth not; charity vaunteth not itself, is not puffed up. Doth not behave itself unseemly, seeketh not her own, is not easily provoked, thinketh no evil."** (1 Corinthians 13:4-8)

My friend let me tell you something: **the lips of another man's wife may be as sweet as honey and her kisses as smooth as olive oil, but when it is all over, she leavens you nothing but bitterness and pain.** Anyone who truly loves you will not endanger your physical and emotional well-being. (Proverbs 5:3-5) Marriage is to be honored by all. Husbands and wives must be faithful to each other. God will judge those who are immoral and those who commit adultery. **Anyone who**

truly cares for you will not tempt you, or jeopardize your relationship with God. Yes! (Hebrews 13:4) In fact if you give into premarital sex you are degrading yourself by giving away something of precious value. (Romans 1:24)

No wonder so many people feel empty and worthless afterward, as if they've carelessly allowed a precious part of themselves to be stolen! Don't let that happen to you. **If someone tries to sweet-talk you into sex by saying, "If you love me, do this," firmly reply, "If you love me, you wouldn't ask!" Your body is too valuable to give away.** Show that you have the strength of character to obey God's command to abstain from fornication. Then, if you do marry someday, you can fully express yourself sexually with your spouse. **And you will be able to enjoy it fully, without the worries, regrets, and insecurities that are so often the aftermath of premarital sex.** (Proverbs 7:22-23; 1 Corinthians 7: 3-5)

Take Note!

(1)   Engaging in premarital sex is an abuse of God's gift. It's like taking a beautiful painting that someone gave you and using it as a doormat.

(2)   Just saying no does not stop the person from asking again. It's how you refuse. If you meekly say no but sound indecisive, it will be obvious. You need to be firm!

(3)   'No,' doesn't always work. Even explaining your beliefs may not work. I've known someone who boasts that they were able to 'break' a Christian. Sometimes you just have to walk away. It's hard to do, but it works.

(4)   As a Christian, you have qualities that will make you attractive to others. So you have to be alert and back off when invited to do something immoral. Respect those qualities. Don't sell out! **Mr. Nicholas. C. Charles,** words: **If you are dating, do you really care for your girlfriend or boyfriend? Then show her\him that you have, the strength to uphold, God's laws, and the wisdom to avoid tempting circumstances.** Read,(Proverbs 22:3; 1 Corinthians 6:18; 13:4-8)

Obedience Protects You!

B—Basic

I—Instruction

B—Before

L—Leaving

E—Earth

[Bible, Come]

C—Children

O—Old ones

M—Middle age

E—Everyone

My friend, change the way you think, and your thinking will change the way you live.

Show me your ways Oh Lord; teach me your paths. Remember not these sins of my youth and my rebellious ways. Good and upright is the Lord therefore he instructs sinners in his ways, the Lord guides the humble in what is right and teaches them his way. Amen!

CHAPTER 20

My Friend, You Need, To Stand Firm in Temptation Times!

Millions of people are faced with temptations everyday. Has anyone ever asked you to do something that was wrong? Were you pressured into doing it? **Were you told that it would be fun and that it was not really wrong to do it?** When someone does this to you, he or she is trying to tempt you. What should you do when you are tempted? Should you give in and do what is wrong? But do you know who would be happy? Yes, Satan, the Devil would be. Satan is the enemy of God, and Satan is your enemy too. **He will tempt you; he would use your friends, family, or even objects. One day Satan himself came and, tried to tempt Jesus.**

My friend, do you know what Jesus did? In the same way, you will know the right thing to do when someone tries to tempt you. **Jesus always wanted to do God's Will.** He openly showed this by being baptized in the Jordan River. It was right after Jesus' baptism, Satan tried to tempt Him. Matthew 3:16-17; 4:1 **tell us that Jesus, after being baptized, was led by the Holy Spirit into the wilderness (desert) to be tempted of the devil.** Forty days and nights went by. During this time Jesus did not eat anything, so he was very, very hungry. **It was at this moment Satan tried to tempt Jesus. Can you imagine? My friend, if you are in a desperate situation, that is the time Satan comes in to tempt you.** For example, if someone is extremely poor, that person might be tempted to steal or do other wrong things to access money and food.

However, God always honor and takes care of the ones who do what's right thing in his name.

The Devil came to Jesus and said, **"If thou be the Son of God, command that these stones be made bread." Jesus was very hungry, so you see a desperate situation existed when Satan came to test him. It was his weakest moment.** But, could Jesus turn stones into bread? Yes, he could have. Why? Because Jesus, the Son of God had special powers. Would you have turned a stone into a loaf of bread if the Devil had asked you to do so? Jesus was hungry. So wouldn't it have been all right to do it just once? No! Jesus knows that it was wrong to use his powers in that way. Instead, Jesus answered and said:

"It is written, man shall not live by bread alone, but by every word that proceedeth out of the mount of God." Jesus knew that doing what pleases God was even more important that having food to eat.

My friend, Satan tried again: "If thou be the Son of God, cast thyself down from this mountain. **For it is written, He shall give his angels charge concerning thee: and in their hands they shall bear thee up, lest at any time thou dash thy foot against a stone.** Jesus said unto Satan, "Thou shalt not tempt the LORD thy God." **People may come to tempt you by misusing the Scriptures. Remember too that Satan tried to test Jesus' understanding of the Scriptures to fool him, therefore some people will do the same, to cause you to fall into error.** But Jesus did not listen to Satan, Instead Jesus responded with other Scriptures: "It is also written: "Thou shalt not tempt the LORD thy God." Jesus knows that it is wrong to tempt God by taking chances with his life. **Still, Satan did not give up. You enemies will not give up, but you must keep strong.**

Satan then took Jesus up on a very high mountain and showed him all the kingdoms on earth and their power and glory saying: **"All these things I will give thee, if thou wilt fall down and worship me."** Someone may not tempt you like that, but they may say, "If you want this job, you have to sleep with me!" What will you do, my friend? **Or on the other hand, a person may not tempt you like that, but they may say**

"**If you sell your soul to the Devil, you will get power, glory and fame, together with lots of money!**" What will you do my friend?

Remember the Devil promised Jesus that same thing, telling him if he worshipped him, he would give him all the power and glory in the world, for his worship (Soul). Jesus knew that it would be wrong to worship the Devil, in spite of what he promised. Jesus answered, "**Get thee hence Satan! "Thou shall worship the LORD thy God, and Him only shalt thou serve.**" (Matthew 4:1-10; Luke 4:1-13) My friend, do the same like Jesus, tell them go away! It is also in the commandment that you shall have no other gods before Him.

The Devil Wants Your Soul; My Friend Say, No!

My friend the Devil will give you success and anything in this world, but the end never is good, this is a promise! **For example, the Devil came to a man, named Devon, and said "I will give you five wishes in exchange for your soul."** The man said, "But my soul is precious, I cannot give you my soul." The Devil said, "Oh really, how do you know that your soul is valuable, **have you ever seen it, what does it do?**" Devon, not knowing replied: "**Well,**" fumbling "**my soul is that, you know, the invisible thing which floats around.**" Suddenly the Devil had an idea, "Do you know Alyssa, the girl of your dreams? **I can make her love you!**"

Devon, being hypnotized by Alyssa after the Devil showed him how happy they could be together, instantly gave in to the Devil's persuasion. **So Devon needing for her to love him, accepted the treacherous offer.** However, he would soon realize that all the wishes which the Devil made come true were conniving, evil and selfish-centered. **The Devil's motive was to make the man gain the whole world and loose his soul, in the Lake of Fire.** (Mark8:38) **My advice:** Never surrender, to anyone who wants to mislead you. Remember the Devil asked Jesus for something he needed, like Devon, and in turn he promised Jesus the world and its greatness. The Devil said, "If you kneel down and worship me."—"All this will I give you."

My friend, if you are into music, acting, or writing and your business associates tells you that they could make you rich and famous, (You can have power, wealth, an attractive mate and virtually anything else you ever dreamed of) but they also goes on to say that you'll only get this success in exchange for your soul, what will you say? **In exchange for your soul simply means worship to a false god for material wealth, which will imprison your mind and your body.** If they succeed they'll make you dress and talk evil and will make you do immoral things. **Remember when you sell your soul they make you commit blasphemy against God and Christian worship.**

The truth is Satan has nothing; he won nothing. And if you want you can be free! I hope you'll say, like Devon, "My soul is precious, and I cannot give that." **What if you're further told that you'll not feel any pain, and you'll not die, for your soul is nothing.** Understand that they are lying to you; you will die and you will feel pain in the lake of fire. **My friend you should answer, "If my soul in nothing, why do you want it?"** You may be further encouraged: "The 'sell soul ritual' just takes a few hours' it is not painful, and souls do not exist." "The whole idea of 'souls' doesn't make any sense; soul doesn't exist. Giving your soul, is just a way of being productive: Making money, finding happiness, looking after yourself and achieving real-life success."

My friend, **Jesus knows that people will come and make perfidious offers, to deceive you.** That is why Jesus said: "**For what shall it profit a man, if he shall gain the whole world, and lose his own soul?**" Or what can a man give in exchange for his soul? If anyone is ashamed of me (Jesus Christ) and my words in this adulterous and sinful generation, the Son of Man will be ashamed of him when he comes in his Father's glory with the holy angels." (Mark 8: 36-38) The man that asked for the soul is lying to you. **Your soul does exist.** What he is saying doesn't make any sense. Why, if souls don't exist, does he want it? Will you want something that doesn't exist?

You must understand, Satan wants you to lose out with God and spend eternity in the 'Lake of Fire' eternally tormented and the only way this can be done is by having your soul. Therefore, he will tell you all kind of treacherous lies, to achieve this purpose. **My friend you should say what Jesus said: "Get thee hence Satan! Thou shall worship the LORD thy God, and Him only shalt thou serve."** (Matthew 4:1-10; Luke 4:1-13) Do the same like Jesus; tell the deceiver to go away with his lies and money. **The biggest mistake people make is to underestimate how badly Satan wants their souls. It's like precious gold to him and he'll pay anything to get it.**

The Meaning of the Illuminati Sell Soul

"Giving your soul" is seen as a way of being productive: Making money, finding happiness, and looking after yourself and achieving real-life success. The 'illuminati' refers to the many secret societies which promote materialism at the cost of one's soul. Didn't Satan promise Jesus that same thing, telling Jesus, if he worshipped him, he would give him all the power and glory in the world, for his worship? (Soul) (Matthew 4:1-10; Luke 4:1-13). Another meaning: **Giving your soul simply means worship to a false god for material wealth, imprisoning your mind and your body, doing whatever the illuminati say to gain wealth and fame, etc.**

My friend, **when you take that offer, your mind and soul is influenced: you cannot see yourself in the light of God. Satan will blind you to make you think that he is the light.** Well, he'll take you to the lake of fire. (2 Corinthians 4:4; 2 Corinthians 11:14-15) **To be free, all you have to do is get on your knees and ask God to forgive you for all your (sins)**

wickedness and evil doings and call on the name of Jesus. Let the Lord be your master and live in your heart. You need to remember Ezekiel 18:4 said "Behold, all souls are mine; as the soul of the father, so also the soul of the son is mine: the soul that sinneth, it shall die." So, your life belongs to God; just call on him. If you don't wish to do that, well, "The soul that sinneth, it shall die." (Ezekiel 18:20)

My friend, **you may feel that the Illuminati is unstoppable—no one can do them anything, no one talks about them—you are wrong. I will expose them, with the power of God.** You may feel that they are all powerful: but they are nothing. "That at the name of Jesus every knee should bow, of things in heaven, and things in earth, and things under the earth; and that every tongue should confess that Jesus Christ is Lord, to the glory of God the Father." (Philippians 2:10-11) **My friend what would you sell your soul for? What is worth eternal fire and damnation? Nothing, yet people do it just for money (wealth, fame, and power).** As I said before, the end will never be good, this is a promise! So change before it is too late.

My friend, the Devil wants your soul. **I beg you, please don't give it to him. The Devil doesn't love you, he wants you to fall out with God and lose eternity life.** He will do anything in his power, to make this happen. He is jealous of God and wants all the glory for himself. That is why; he comes to offer you life's success; **because your soul is precious and it belongs** to God. **God sent his Son Jesus to die for you and the Devil wants all of this to be in vain.** God placed a soul in every man in order to become alive and to rule the earth through God's law. **Never say the Devil cannot come to oppose you, because Satan has power enough to oppose even the angels in heaven.** (Jude 9; Daniel 10:12-13), so who are you? What does it profit you if you gain the whole world but lose your soul? (Mark 8: 36-38)

The Selfish Devil!

The Devil wants your soul, because he doesn't want to be in the lake of fire by himself, he wants you there with him. **He is selfish (yeah, yeah, he is!) He is jealous of you because, of your relationship with God. Because you** have power through Jesus Christ, as the Bible said: "Behold, I give unto you the power to tread on serpents and scorpions, and over all the power of the enemy: and nothing shall by any means hurt you." (Luke 10: 19) **That is why Satan wants your soul! The Devil wants to be in control, he wants to take your power, in Jesus Christ. But he can't, if you don't allow him and even self you allow him call on Jesus He will restore you.**

My friend, God has provided the means of defending yourselves against Satan's attacks. He said! "Put on the whole armor of God that ye may be able to stand against the wiles of the devil." "For we wrestle not against flesh and blood, but against principalities, against powers, against rulers of the darkness of this world, against spiritual wickedness in high places: **Wherefore take unto you the whole armor of God that ye may be able to withstand in the evil days, and having done all, to stand.**" (Ephesians 6:11-12) My friend, do you know that there are so many people giving the Devil their soul, and not knowing it; **my friend the Devil is taking people (your) soul through some of the radio programs, television shows, videos and books etc.**

Destroying your faith, Satan is so foolish; his power is limited by God's will. The temptations in your life are no different from what others experience. And God is faithful! He will not allow the temptation to be more than you can bear. **When you are tempted, he will show you a way out so that you can endure; you have more power than Satan, which is why Satan wants you badly.** (Job 1:10-12; 1 Corinthians 10:13) **My friend, without Christ, you (we) are all under condemnation of death.** (Romans 3:23) Before you are saved, you are in bondage to the Devil, as (1 John 5:19) says, **"The whole world lies in the power of the Evil One." Praise the Lord, You have a new Master (Jesus Christ), the One who can break the chains of any sin and set (You) us free.** (1 Corinthians 6:9-11; Mark 5:1-15)

You are free! Amen! My friend the Devil only has dominion over those who live without Christ in the world. As the Bible says "In whom the god of this world hath blinded the minds of them which believe not, lest the light of the glorious gospel

of Christ, who is the image of God, should shine unto them."
(2 Corinthians 4:4) **When you are tempted, he will show you
a way out so that you can endure; you have more power than
Satan, which is why Satan wants you badly.** (Job 1:10-12; 1
Corinthians 10:13) **My friend, without Christ, you (we) are
all under condemnation of death.** (Romans 3:23) Before you
are saved, you are in bondage to the Devil, as (1 John 5:19)
says, **"The whole world lies in the power of the Evil One."**

Praise the Lord, **You have a new Master (Jesus Christ),
the One who can break the chains of any sin and set (You)
us free.** (1 Corinthians 6:9-11; Mark 5:1-15) **You are free!
Amen!** My friend the Devil only has dominion over those
who live without Christ in the world. As the Bible says **"In
whom the god of this world hath blinded the minds of them
which believe not, lest the light of the glorious gospel of
Christ, who is the image of God, should shine unto them."**
(2 Corinthians 4:4) That is why, those that sell their soul for
money, wealth and fame, etc., Cannot see themselves in the
light of God.

**Satan has blinded them, making them think, that he is
the light. Meanwhile, he is taking them to the lake of fire.** No
wonder the Bible said Satan himself masquerades as an angel of
light. And he is also using men and women, to mislead people,
as the Bible said. **"And no marvel; for Satan transformed into
an angel of light.** Therefore it is no great thing if his ministers
also be transformed as the ministers if righteousness; whose

end shall be according to their works." **Their end will be what their actions deserve. As I say, this is a promise: the end will never be good** (2 Corinthians 11:14-15)

Evil Spirit Obeys God's People!

My friend, accept Jesus Christ today! **You know the truth, do you remember the slave girl who had a spirit of divination and brought her owners much gain by fortune-telling.** When she saw men of God, she cried out, **"These men are servants of the Most High God, which shew unto us the way of salvation."** (So those evil spirits know the truth when they hear it. Do you want salvation?) I say to the evil spirit now in you, "I command thee in the name of Jesus Christ to come out of her." **My friends believe that you are free, in the name of Jesus Christ.** (Acts 16:16-19; 8:9-11) **Now repent, then, of this evil plan, and pray to the Lord that he will forgive you for thinking such a thing as this for I see that you are full of bitter envy and are a prisoner of sins.** (Acts 8:22)

My friend, when the Devil takes your soul, you are a prisoner. You may say no because you can eat and drink, go anyway you want, and do anything you wish, but you are wrong. **You will not enter the kingdom of God. Your soul is kept as a prisoner, and Satan is just waiting to kill you, so that you can go to the "Lake of Fire" with him.** My advice: Please read Isaiah 14:12-15, it is very important; you will see Satan for who he really is. My friend, I have shown my point already. **If I miss** out on anything, that I should say, and to learn more you can email me at: **truthofsalvation463@ymail.com** or add me to Skype, name **Jesusiscomingyou.** Do you know some of the temptations we are also faced with? Here are some examples: sex, lies, alcohol and drugs.

For example: your mother may have money in her cashbox. And she tells you don't take her money and do not go anywhere. **But at this same moment a friend calls you and say, let us go and lime somewhere.** What will you do, in this case? My friend, **you will feel temped to take the money even if your mother says don't take it.** Will you obey your mother or your friends? The tempter, Satan wants you to disobey her, remember Jesus obeyed God his father. He knows that pleasing God was more important than anything in this world. You show that you are like Jesus when you do what your mother says. **It may be that some of your friends will ask you; do you want to go by some girls to have sex with them?** They may also say, it will make you feel really good, but having sex out of marriage will not please God. On the other hand, you could get be afflicted with a sexual disease.

My friend, what about if you friend give you a cigarette, which also contains drugs, and dare you to smoke it. What will you do? **If your boyfriend or girlfriend asks you to come home by them to have sexual relationship with them, what will you do? If one of your friend asks you to go with them by friends to drink alcohol and smoke drugs, what will you** do? Remember Jesus. Satan tried to get Jesus to take chances with his life by telling him to jump off the temple. **But Jesus did not do such a foolish thing like that. What will you do if someone asks you to do something dangerous?** What you should do, my friend? Jesus did not listen to Satan. Neither should you listen to anyone who tries to get you to do wrong things.

Will you perform an act of worship before an image, or idol, something the Bible says you must not do? Let us read together at. Exodus 20:4-5 says "Thou shalt have no other gods before me. **Thou shalt not make into thee any graven image, or any likeness of any things that is in heaven above, or that is in the earth beneath, or that is in water under the earth.**" My friend this is a world of wickedness, and full of temptations. So be strong! My friend, even if the act of worship is part of a ceremony at church or school. You may be told that you cannot even go to church or school anymore if you refuse to do this. What will you do? **It is easy to do what is right when everyone else is doing it.**

But doing what is right can be pretty hard when others are trying to get us to do wrong. **They may say that what they are doing is not really bad.** But the big question is what does God say about it? He knows best! **So no matter what others say, you should never do things that God says are wrong.** In that way you will always make God happy and you will never please the Devil. **To give you some encouragement, I will** tell you about three men, who was tempted and refused to worship and act of images, and for doing this, the Most High rewarded them.

Shadrach, Meshach, and Abednego refused to worship king Nebuchadnezzar gods and golden statue, and the king said to Meshach, Abednego and Shadrach: "**If you don't worship my gods and golden statue which I set up when you hear the music, I will throw you into the flaming furnace.**" Do you know what the king said? "No god can save you from me." The three men replied, "**Your Majesty, we don't need to defend ourselves. The God we worship can save us from you and your flaming furnace. But even if he doesn't, we still won't worship your gods and the gold statue you have set up.**" Can you hear these men faith, and encouragement? The king did throw them into the flaming furnace, do you know God protect them from the furnace. If you want to LEARN more read (Daniel 3:1-30)

Shadrach, Meshach, Abednego want to tell you something wonderful. My friend, you should know that God loves you very much, under any circumstances. **He does think of you and will always protect you from temptations and evil men, whom Satan uses to tempt us. To learn more about how to resist temptations, look at:** Psalm 1:1-2; Proverbs 1:10-11; Matthew 26:41 and 2 Timothy 2:22) When you get some time, read these Scriptures, and understand them: (Luke 21.30-36; Luke 6.39-40,41-45,46-49; Luke 9.25,55-56,60;

Luke 8.5-8,10-17' Luke 4.4; Revelation 22.13-17; Genesis 11.1,3-9; 1 Timothy 6.7; Luke 12.29-32; Luke 10.24-26,28; Luke 24.44-45,47-48; Luke 11.33-36,46-52; Leviticus 4.13,22; Matthew 22.17-21,32; Exodus 20.12; Luke 10.20; Exodus 20.1-18; Exodus 23.24,32.

Your Chance to Repent and Walk in God's Wisdom!

These are just a few important principles which have been shared with you in the book, "From Worldly to Christian Wisdom and Truth." **Following these principles of heaven will bring you into a fuller appreciation and understanding of your Creator and Lord and Saviour, Jesus Christ.** Your borders will be enlarged as you begin to benefit from the divine favour and blessings which result from you obedience to God's word, which is designed to bring you into true liberty and fulfilment.

Maybe, you are someone who has never made Jesus Christ your Lord and Saviour, or, after reading this book, you would now like to recommit your life to God. Why not pray with me?

"Lord Jesus, I have just read about your principles of life in this book. I thank you for using your messenger, to impart Your wisdom into my life. **I now repent of my old ways and thoughts to embrace you unfailing word.** Forgive me for my former lifestyle of rebellion to your will, Lord Jesus. **I turn from**

rebellion to obedience and cooperation. Let your kingdom, your influence, your authority and reign now come upon my life, Lord, and let Your will be done. **I receive You, Lord Jesus, as my Lord and Master and will walk in your ways from this day on; in the power of Your Holy Spirit.** Amen."

Friend, if you have prayed this prayer with an honest heart, I declare that you are now a child of God! **"But as many as received him, to them gave he power to become the sons of God, even to them that believe on his name."** (John 1:12-15) Study God's word and walk in obedience to His will.

Blessings
Messenger,
Nicholas C Charles

[About the Messenger]

Mr. Nicholas C Charles is a visionary writer who has a mountain of faith-in God and towards his books. He carries the pure and (raw) message of God. My friend, it is Mr. Charles' divine calling to be a writer and preacher. **Furthermore he is a young inspirational leader to those in authority and the youths in his community.**

Mr. Charles is stern in his calling to become a world-class writer and preacher. **Mr. Charles is one who aspires to be the best father and husband.** *Also, in all the roles of life, he aspires to be the best he can be; as a parent, a son, a husband, a brother, a friend and most important, a man of God. He also acquires the persistence and determination of being a writer in the midst of constant adversities.* **He is hard working and focused on heavenly things.**

Being saved at a tender age, **he immediately knew he was destined to be a writer, and a preacher.** *While still in secondary (high) school, Mr. Charles preached the gospel to his peers; even to teachers. Many opposed him, along with the God he served.* **Mr. Charles struggled to be accepted within many social institutions, due to the preaching of the gospel and has been persecuted and rejected by loved ones even before becoming 18 years of age.**

Adversities have all worked out in his favor as whom God blesses let no man curse. *"No weapon that is formed against thee (him) shall prosper; and every tongue that shall rise against thee (him) in judgment thou shalt condemn." (Isaiah 54:17)* **I want to encourage any servant of God who is being persecuted to remember these messages and hold on. God has your future in the very palm of his hands and has your blessings in the center of his heart.** *"Casting all your care upon him; for he careth for* **you."** *(1 Peter 5:7) I love you!*

My advice!

My friend: Do not let anyone look down on you or think less of you because you are young, but let your light shine, in your conduct, towards them, in love, in faith, in charity, and purity. (1 Timothy 4:12) **I give these instructions to you, receive them and you shall be a good servant of Christ. Go and do what I have commanded you!** *"Remember now thy Creator in the days of thy youth, while* *the evil days come not, nor the years draw nigh, when thou shalt say; **I have no pleasure in them.**" (Ecclesiastes 12:1)*

Witten by
Lurissa Sookdeo

ACKNOWLEDGMENT

All Praise is due to the Heavenly Father. First and foremost, I thank God. I praise Him because, if it were not for His Gregariousness, this helpful tool to you would never have materialized. **I express my thanks to you O, God for giving me the strength to accomplish this task. I love you, God with all of my soul. I will never compromise you in anything, even if my life depended on it.** Reader, remember this book is already prescribed for you by God.

It is an honor to call you, my Pastor, Pastor Julien Cyrus. **I honestly express my gratitude to you for your hard work and dedication to the success of this manuscript.** Pastor Julien Cyrus played a vital part in preparing this book for publication. **I can distinguish this man from the other teachers I know. He is a Godsend to me!** May God reward you accordingly on judgment day. May God fulfill the good pleasure of His will in your life.

And shall I not thank my dear wife Lurissa, for her co-operation, financial support and encouragement. Thanks for your prayers, your love and passion. **You're an inspiration to me, thank you with all of my heart, love you!** Lurissa you are my sister, my friend, and my love, thank you for being there, in my hard times, but instead of adding to my hardship, you've supported me by showing your unconditional love. **I am truly grateful for that, one love!**

To my mother, Cheryl Lawrence, who raised me up in the absence of a father-figure: Thank you for your words of wisdom. I love you. You may not understand it, but if you look into the depths of your heart you'll see my love for you, Mom. **Thanks for being there and not giving up on me, when you felt like doing it. Thanks for continually praying for me; thanks a million. There are no words to express all my gratitude for you.** I HEREBY SAY, THANKS. I know you are very proud of me now. **May God bring you to the place He's ordained for you. Amen!**

Acknowledgement is also in order for my dear friend, **Mr. Wade Hinkson. I am thrilled to call you, my father. You supported me till the very end.** Mr. Hinkson, I am grateful for being my help when I did not see any help; you know what I am talking about. I do not know what to say to you again;

I am so overjoyed. **Mr. Hinkson, God richly bless you with eternal life.**

Thanks to all others who contributed towards this book. I feel that they would prefer to remain unknown. **God knows them and I ask Him to reward them with eternal life in heaven.** Thanks to all of you! Amen!

Written by The messenger, N C Charles

Bibliography

And Some Additional Information from YouTube and on the Internet.